Untrain
Your
Parrot

Untrain Your Parrot

And Other No-Nonsense Instructions on the Path of Zen

Elizabeth Hamilton

Shambhala

BOSTON & LONDON 2007

Shambhala Publications, Inc.
Horticultural Hall
300 Massachusetts Avenue
Boston, Massachusetts 02115
www.shambhala.com

9 8 7 6 5 4 3 2 1
First Edition
Printed in the United States of America

♾ This edition is printed on acid-free paper that meets
the American National Standards Institute z39.48 Standard.
Distributed in the United States by Random House, Inc.,
and in Canada by Random House of Canada Ltd.

Designed by Dede Cummings Designs

Library of Congress Cataloging-in-Publication Data
Hamilton, Elizabeth, 1942–
Untrain your parrot: and other no-nonsense instructions on
the path of Zen / Elizabeth Hamilton; foreword by Rosa Parks.
    p.   cm.
Includes index.
ISBN 978-1-59030-363-4 (alk. paper)
1. Zen Buddhism—Doctrines. 2. Spiritual life—Zen Buddhism.
I. Title.
BQ9268.3.H36 2007
294.3'420427—dc22
2006103234

To Helen and Clint Hamilton
and Mother Rosa Parks

Contents

Foreword

ELIZABETH'S HEARTFELT WORDS and meditations at our conventions and public presentations in Mexico and Canada and in Detroit and Los Angeles have kept everyone heedful of the need for self-development and valuing all diversities. Her presentations reflect the kindness and empowerment that are so necessary for our youth, and for one another.

These efforts are the foundation on which our ability to serve life rests. Elizabeth's ongoing service leadership and volunteer efforts serve our continuing effort to bring about what Dr. King called the Beloved Community. Keep up the great work!

Rosa Parks

Full is empty, this is true,
You are me and I am you.

M. T. HEAD

Preface

Untraining your parrot is the direct path to unconditioned living.
M. T. HEAD

WHEN I BECAME A ZEN student thirty years ago I hoped naively that zen's vast emptiness would be the perfect antidote for my existential "dis-ease." Truthfully, what I expected to happen was that I'd still feel like the same old me, without some of my more egregious flaws. So it came as a shock when the very self that I was planning to fix up began to deconstruct, at times subtly, at times volcanically.

Much of what I had considered unique about me turned out to be the musings of a well-trained parrot, deeply ingrained conditioned views that I, like everyone, had acquired in the process of trying to be a somebody. This isn't bad; it's just too bad, since we hold onto this Gospel of Myself as if it were a life raft. We may not realize how much trouble it causes us, and others, when we engage in conduct that is often described in terms of bird behaviors: ruffled feathers, henpecking, ruling the roost, and pecking order.

Our determination to acquire and train our varied identities reminds me of my third-grade year, when my dad, just back from combat in Korea, brought home forty parakeets and installed them in a huge aviary in the backyard. The image of all those birds, and their endless babies, reminds me of our own virtual aviary of identities, each with its specific plumage and birdcalls. All that squawking makes it hard to hear the quiet warblings tenderly emanating from the heart of our being.

We should never underestimate the persistence of our parrot. Part of the process of awakening involves recognizing the many identities we have acquired. I'm still occasionally tempted to identify myself as a professional musician because I've been performing on the harpsichord for forty years. Likewise, three decades of involvement with zen prompts an urge to don the mantle of "zen personage." How many times have you asked, "What do you *do*?" when you first meet someone? Could it be that our enthusiasm for identity acquisition signifies our unwillingness to enter the unboundedness of the unknown?

Now that my great future is behind me, the process of assembling the materials in this book has prompted my well-trained parrot, which usually seems to be more of a pet than a pest, to try to reinstate its illusion of control. One old favorite tune, "Be sure to sound as if you're in the know" has reauditioned as "Be sure to tie anything that might sound un-zen-like to some unassailable classic zen tenet." The ego parrot has no compunctions about co-opting the language of wakefulness; then, caught in the act, it turns tail and says, "You should know better by now!" Fortunately we've been bestowed with a sense of humor, and ample doses will be required when we see what we've been up to, and how much is yet to be learned, and unlearned.

Zen reminds us that our enterprise isn't one of reconditioning; it's one of meeting the unconditioned, of encountering the inexpressible nature of existence that is common to all. This process, which occurs organically through applied awareness, constitutes most of the contents of this book, with applications that address the wide spectrum of human perception and functioning. Zen training is bound to bring up fear and resistance. But the only things that are truly dispelled as we travel the path of awakening are our incomplete and inaccurate views of things, the glue that keeps our programming intact. And then guess what? As everything falls away, paradoxically we get it all back; that's part of zen's message of oneness, of the "inter-being" of all existence.

We may feel as if we're caught in quicksand when we first hear zen's constant reminders that there is no self, and nothing but the self, but such phrases are best considered as koans to plop into, just as Basho's famous haiku frog plopped into a pond centuries ago. Even as we aspire to selflessness, we'll need a provisional sense of self to take care of practical matters. However, this provisional, or relative-world, self doesn't have to limit our ineffable nature.

Our inquiry will revolve around the five dimensions of heartmind and the seeds of awakening, terms that may sound unfamiliar, yet their components will be recognizable as they are introduced. Appreciating that we need all the help we can get, I've filled this volume with what I hope are helpful tools, exercises, and meditation practices for bringing the formal teachings of zen into our everyday experience.

By the way, while most of my formal training has been in zen, I've been profoundly affected by the commonality that shines forth in diverse spiritual heritages. Hopefully this book reflects the transdenominationality and universality that resound in many traditions. It is intended for those of all persuasions, or none, and to honor this inclusivity, I'll use a lower-case z for zen, except in titles of works and in proper names.

Using language to discuss zen is a delicate balancing act. When grammatical conventions meet subject matter relating to the interpenetrating, interdependent nature of existence, caution is required. For years I've tried to minimize possessive pronouns and subject-verb-object linguistic structure, which reinforce illusions of ownership and doer-ship, as in the sentence "When *I* 'do' meditation, *I* pay attention to *my* breathing." Still, omitting the I's and me's won't convince the ego to relinquish its imperious claims. I've also found that nondual language makes for stilted, disembodied, and even self-conscious writing. Hopefully the conventional grammatical structures here won't be construed as an invitation to engage in *doing zen* instead of *being zen.*

Speaking of words, those that are now part of the English language, like *koan, zen, sesshin,* and *chi kung,* will follow English language conventions.

One caveat: don't believe anything you read in these pages. My approach is to act as a guide, and if I hold any definition as a zen teacher, it is that of practitioner, learner, and occasional tour guide or practice consultant. Further, anything in these pages that sounds like a belief system should be regarded as a hypothesis to serve as an experiment in the laboratory of awakening. Scholars, historians, translators, and philosophers will recognize that I'm none of these. My ongoing research occurs primarily on a meditation seat and in applied daily-life practice, guided by the yearning to penetrate, and be interpenetrated by, reality. All of us are qualified to engage in this venture.

All errors of comprehension are mine. Sincere apologies to the spiritual ancestors of the heritages I have cited, for whatever misperceptions I have made concerning the message they wished to impart. My confidence is with the reader, as we journey through the fields of the five dimensions of heartmind and discover the seeds of awakening that are already planted there, assisted by zen's vows to minimize harm, live beneficially, and awaken to our fundamental unity.

1 What's Most Important?

Heartmind has the totality of space: nothing lacking, nothing extra.
SENG-TS'AN, THIRD ZEN ANCESTOR, D. 606

ONE DAY ALFRED NOBEL opened the newspaper and was shocked to find his obituary: "Alfred Nobel, the inventor of dynamite, died this week." Actually, his brother had died; however, the realization that his legacy would be the invention of dynamite prompted Alfred to do some soul searching. Examining what he considered to be most important led to his developing the Nobel Peace Prize, which joined his deepest values with his resources to honor humankind's efforts on behalf of world peace and cooperation.

If you died today, would your obituary reflect your professed values? Or entropy: "She let the important things slide, and then she died." The obituary question invites us to reflect on whether the things we consider most important are echoed in our use of time, money, and energy.

The question isn't just "What's important to me?"—which is likely to veer toward self-centered responses; it's "What's most important, from an all-encompassing, life-centered, or reality-centered perspective?" After all, life is life-centered rather than *self*-centered, unlike people.

One way of stating what's most important might be: to awaken wholeheartedly to the wisdom and compassion of our actual nature and to live in accord with it. That's a lot of loaded words. *Wisdom* is seeing life face-to-face. *Compassion* involves living in alignment with the fundamental interconnectedness that wisdom reveals, which naturally manifests as loving-kindness. There's reinforcement from all sides, inviting us to wake up. Greek writer-philosopher Nikos Kazantzakis describes the vastness around us: "Blowing through heaven and earth, and in our hearts and in the heart of every living thing, is a gigantic breath—a great cry—which we call God."[*]

Christians speak of the Kingdom of God within and the Kingdom of Heaven at hand;[†] the Qur'an says, "Whithersoever ye turn, there is the presence of God, for God is all-pervading;"[‡] and Buddhism regularly refers to our very body as the body of Buddha (awakening), and to this very land as the Lotus Land, or our true home.[§] The message is consistent, no matter what we call it—God, love, enlightenment, oneness, or Paradise—the actuality is all-encompassing and ineffable. However, our

---

[*] Nikos Kazantzakis, *Report to Greco* (New York: Simon & Schuster, 1961).
[†] Ephesians 5:26.
[‡] Holy Qur'an 2:115, trans. Abdullah Yusuf Ali (Beltsville, Md.: Amana Publishers, 1999.)
[§] Zen Center San Diego Service Book.

approach to discerning this firsthand can't be ineffable if things are to move from abstract philosophy to a juicy, vital reality. We need to proceed in as straightforward and practical a manner as possible, so spiritual practices usually develop methods, called *upaya* or "skillful means" in Sanskrit.

It takes aspiration, perspiration, and sometimes desperation for these dimensions and seeds of awakening to be cultivated and to bloom. Fortunately, we don't have to make any pilgrimages elsewhere, since what's most important is already revealed, right here.

Zen: Awakening Heartmind

Although living in accord with what's most important doesn't require historical study, some background on zen and one of its parents, Buddhism, may be helpful. Buddhism, like most world religions, is characterized by cultural, ceremonial, hierarchical, and gender associations, along with specific beliefs, such as karma and rebirth. Although born as a Hindu, the best-known non-Buddhist, Shakyamuni Buddha, got his name when someone asked him who he was, and he replied that he was "the Awakened One," which is the *Buddha* in Sanskrit.

Bodhidharma, who is considered the founder of the Zen (or Chan) tradition, was an elusive Indian Buddhist monk who went to China, encountered Taoists and martial artists, and developed a discipline he called *Chan*. The word *chan*, a transliteration of the Sanskrit word *dhyana*, or meditation for the sake of awakening to reality, was originally used in Hinduism. Zen, the Japanese equivalent, has now entered the English vernacular. Bodhidharma referred to Chan as "a teaching . . . not relying on preaching or scriptures, pointing directly to heartmind."* Traditional Chinese medicine confirms the need for heartmind to be activated, as a primary remedy for diminished physical, emotional, and spiritual vitality.

Like many meditative traditions, zen draws people from diverse backgrounds and has developed comfortable affiliations with Judaism, Christianity, Taoism, martial arts, nationalism, visual arts, poetry, scholarship, and rambunctiousness. We all bring our predilections along, and that's no problem, as long as they remain condiments to flavor the main dish: waking up to what we already are.

Sometimes people ask how the Zen Center of San Diego (ZCSD), the meditation center where my partner, Ezra, and I teach, can be *zen* without being denominationally Buddhist; aren't they one and the same? Not necessarily; many zen groups are Buddhist, yet a fair number consider themselves Christian or nondenominational, like ZCSD, rather than being religiously affiliated. This catholicity accords with Bodhidharma's teachings, as best I can tell, given his de-emphasis on the centrality of scriptures, his willingness to consult with Taoists, and his Buddhist roots. It appears that his primary concern was to help students awaken to the shared reality inherent in our existence, which applies equally to all.

One of my early teachers, Taizan Maezumi Roshi, a primary figure among Japanese Zen Buddhists who have come to America, presided over the ceremony in which I undertook Zen's precepts for living compassionately, "as if awake." While the rites involved were prescribed by his Japanese Zen Buddhist tradition, he hospitably acknowledged my resolve to be a

---

* *Hsin* or *xin* in Chinese refers to the mind whose residence is in the heart; in Sanskrit, *bodhicitta* is the word for "the compassionate heart of the awakened mind." Both terms attest to the need for our head and heart to be hooked up, for the compassion of clear seeing and heartmind to walk in our shoes.

"life monk," rather than committing to follow any particular individual c
religion. Publicly affirming such vows honors an interior calling, much ₂
marriage confirms a relationship that is already in process. I deeply appreciate his compassionate confirmation of the universality of our practice.

In this same spirit, when the Zen Center of San Diego first started, and
I was the resident monk, we used readings from the Zen Center of Los Angeles, Japanese Zen master Shunryu Suzuki, Chögyam Trungpa Rinpoche,
a Tibetan Buddhist teacher, universally oriented teacher-writer Stephen
Levine, and Catholic mystic Meister Eckhart, among others. Occasionally
participants would ask, "Where's the zen?" The answer resounds in the
readings themselves. I was first inspired to practice zen in a way that transcends sectarian boundaries when I heard a talk by Catholic Trappist monk
Thomas Merton. He suggested that rather than being about beliefs and
rites, Buddhism is concerned with opening to love.

Confirming What's Real Where and When?

What does it take to verify our deepest aspiration (what's most important)
experientially, and then have it come alive in the monastery of daily life? At
age eighteen, I got a powerful wake-up jolt that brought this question to
my attention when my grandfather, a respected Christian preacher, fal-
tered in his faith during his last year of life. He announced that he no
longer believed in God, didn't think much of people, and had no expectations of going to heaven, since he now doubted its existence—all the things
that had been most important to him. And then he died. Sorrowfully, the
very beliefs that had provided solace during his lifetime fell away precipitously, just when they would have been most applicable, his preaching having focused largely on life after death.

My grandpa's legacy turned out to be a mandate to me to question all of my assumptions. His turnaround confirmed that belief alone isn't enough, since it can change in a flash. Besides, if one person's change of beliefs could affect ultimate reality, wouldn't the consequences be catastrophic? What had changed was his mind, and that's what minds do—they change. We've all stood witness to the dissolution of deeply etched beliefs.

Contemplating this stilled my concerns about what might happen to Grandpa after his death, as my inquiry eventually shifted from speculation about life after death to the vital matter of life *before* death. I felt an upwelling of empathy for those whose lives seem so agonizing that an afterlife appears to be the only bearable option. As a Christian at the time, certain Biblical phrases that I'd ignored began to pique my curiosity. For instance, what does the Gospel of Matthew's "If thine eye be single, the whole body shall be filled with light" mean?* What is this single, or unified, eye? What fills the body with light? Do you have to wait until after death to see the light? I was still fixated on what happens after death, or up ahead. This focus on the future, rather than the present, is symptomatic of a malady that can plague us for a lifetime, *until-itis*: we attend secondary school *until* college; we go to college *until* a job or marriage comes along; we pursue a spiritual practice *until* we get results. The mantra of until-itis is "Where will this get me?" *Until, until, until.* We seemingly put life on hold, even as it unfolds, *until* we die.

Years after my grandfather's death, I questioned Maezumi Roshi, "What do *you* think happens when you die?" Smiling, he said, "Uh oh! You'd better ask someone dead!" That's the best advice I'd had about com-

* Matthew 6:22.

prehending life after death. He also said later, "One understanding of li
and death is the life and death of the instant. According to Dogen Zenji, 'I..
twenty-four hours our life is born and dying.'"* Later, I spent a few months
with Ram Dass, who might best be described as a humanitarian universal-
ist. During one conversation, his response to my question about death was
"If you're here now, you'll be there then."

When we're caught up with concerns about things that haven't happened yet, it's hard to stay in touch with what's most important now.
Sometimes it takes a serious illness or the loss of a loved one to rearrange
our priorities and knock our speculations out from under us. Yet if and
when we recover, the great forgetting may resume rapidly, again side-
lining our concern for contacting what's most important in the present
moment.

Unlike Alfred Nobel, we don't have to wait until our obituary confronts
us to consider our inmost wish. If we have time to read this, we must have
the good fortune of life circumstances that permit time to raise existential
questions.

Should we take things on faith as we attempt to discern what's most important to us? Not in the sense of beliefs or of blindly accepting something
we're told. Our basic job description involves learning to stay present, to see
things as they really are, ourselves included, and to attend to what seems to
block awakening wholeheartedly to whatever situation is at hand.

We seem to have an inherent compass that is attuned to a spiritual itch,
no matter how dormant it may be. This isn't the same as the homing urge
of the swallows here in Southern California, who return home to Capis-

* Taizan Maezumi, *Appreciate Your Life*, Wendy Egyoku Nakao and Eve Myonen
Marko (Boston: Shambhala Publications, 2001).

trano the same time every year, without requiring any training to do so. Rather, Zen assures us that we're already home; we just haven't noticed.

Speaking of birds, I learned a lot about the extent to which my own programming blocked awareness when we brought our baby birds, Otis and Little Richard, home from the bird orphanage. I wanted to teach them to talk, the way the baby birds I had trained as a youngster had done, but they bonded to each other instead of to me. Finally I stopped trying to teach them to say "Be here" and started listening to them. Hearing the richness and variety of their songs, I realized that my endeavor had been tantamount to trying to teach John Coltrane and Miles Davis to sing a pop tune like Johnny One Note.

Zen is more a case of untraining than training, of encountering the unconditioned rather than acquiring new conditioning. As our parrot is untrained, we may find that we are already at our true home, the place of heartmind.

What's Most Important: A Worksheet

Write down a short statement of what you consider to be the point of spiritual practice, and what you consider most important—from an all-encompassing, life-centered perspective—as of now.

1. Now spend about five minutes writing a list of additional thoughts concerning what's most important to you, without pausing to evaluate your notes. The order of importance doesn't matter; put down whatever comes up.

2. Next, consider which of the following motivations speak to your interest in spiritual involvement most strongly. Circle the items that are most significant to you:

   - encountering ultimate reality
   - living constructively
   - meeting a guide for your quest
   - awakening compassion
   - healing long-standing pain
   - finding something to believe in
   - associating with like-minded people
   - looking for a family or partner
   - discovering something that transcends your sense of self
   - looking for solace from loneliness or alienation
   - other: write in any other motivations that occur to you

3. Return to your two lists with a highlighter in hand, and mark those items that seem charged in some way. It doesn't matter whether they seem shallow or out of sequence; honesty is what matters. Coffee and a banana are high on my list of motivations, since they help get me out of bed and into the meditation hall every morning.

4. Assess whether the things you have indicated as most important are reflected in the way you live and in your allocation of time, energy, and other resources. This isn't about applause or an indictment; it's simply an opportunity to consider whether your values and daily activities are in alignment. If some of the answers are shocking, that's a good thing to know.

2 The Five Dimensions of Heartmind

Everythin' is somethin', and somethin' is no-thin', And no-thin' is a bunch—at noon we call it lunch.

M. T. HEAD, *HIPHOP HEART SUTRA*

THE STORY "WHAT AM I Leaving Out?" by Benedictine Father Theophane Boyd,* concerns a young monk who arrives at a monastery late one night and tells the abbot that he is desperate for enlightenment. Refusing the abbot's suggestion that he get some rest, he requests a theme to contemplate overnight in the chapel. The abbot suggests "What am I leaving out?" and retires, whereupon the agitated monk forgoes meditation and goes in search of answers. He knocks on the doors of the monks' cells, waking up each monk to ask, "What am I

---

* Father Theophane Boyd, "What Am I Leaving Out?" in *Tales of a Magic Monastery* (New York: Crossroads Publishing, 1981).

leaving out?" Each monk responds, "Me!" Finally he falls to the floor, crying, "What am I leaving out?" The floor says, "Me." He runs out into the night, and cries to the moon, "What am I leaving out?" "Me!"

All of those "me's" add up, and we can easily leave out, or ignore, many valuable people, places, and events on our journey of awakening and discerning what's most important. Since awakening isn't likely to be an all-at-once thing, usually being gradual and situational, having a practical road map for consultation helps ensure that nothing essential falls through the cracks.

The road map we will use for discovering what's before our eyes will be the *five dimensions of heartmind:* the physical, mental, emotional, open awareness, and full-empty dimensions described below.

1. Physical. The physical dimension considers the world of objects, bodily sensations, sensory phenomena, movement, chi (energy), and activity.

2. Mental. The mental dimension is the broad range of mind functions, from clear thinking to clearly deluded thinking, from objective description to subjective opinions and beliefs. Here we find the *sixth sense,* Buddhist cosmology's term for the objective thinking that describes what is perceived mindfully.*

3. Emotional. The emotional dimension reflects moods, states of mind, and reactions to events.

4. Open awareness. Like an invisible picture frame, the open awareness dimension holds whatever we perceive. At first open awareness is colored by a perception of dividedness, as if something were watching something else, a relic of our old habit of splitting seamless reality. A useful side

---

* *Shambhala Dictionary of Buddhism and Zen* (Boston: Shambhala Publications, 1991).

effect of this is that it makes it possible for the *observer,* or objective awareness, to function consciously. The observer provides a context for the *experiencer,* or our capacity for embodied sentient perception. At first, these seem separate, with the observer seeming somehow environmental or outside the skin, while the experiencer seems confined to bodily sensations. As these functions unite, we start to sample empirical evidence of spaciousness and of our inter-being with existence.

5. *Full-empty. Full* refers to life's vastness and inclusivity, with no need for names; *empty* indicates the absence of any fixed quality or solidity. Full-empty isn't precisely a dimension; rather, it's the primordial nature of all of the dimensions, weaving everything into the insubstantial tapestry of existence. Zen uses terms like form-is-emptiness and absolute-is-relative to refer to the insubstantiality that undergirds the seemingly tangible stuff of life. *Absolute* is synonymous with the empty aspect of full-emptiness, and *relative* describes the appearances it takes in the world of form. These are united in full-emptiness.

Full-emptiness is numinous, impermanent, unknowable—and it's what we are. Because of full-emptiness, zen and other nondual traditions can say, with noetic conviction, that there's no self and nothing but the self. Experiential brushes with this dimension can be incandescent, and they immediately distinguish the path of awakening from the lessons of self-help, philosophy, and psychology. The mystery of full-emptiness may open fleetingly, with or without spiritual practice: you're sitting in the park and a birdsong shimmers right through your torso, obliterating the dividing lines that make objects seem separate. You are ensconced in unutterable wonder, until someone walks up and irritably asks if that's your damn dog that's running loose, whereupon you're plopped back into the me-versus-them mentality we know so well.

Misty landscapes of zen paintings attempt to depict this full-empty realm, yet they can't convey the palpable living warmth that blooms as this dimension awakens. Not surprisingly, the ego may find it more awful than awe-full when intimations of the full-empty realm start to emerge; it intuits that these hints of some other way of seeing things might just dismantle its assumptions of primacy. A particle physicist who meditates told me that when his lab mates realized that the insubstantiality of the quantum quarks and charms they were seeing under the microscope included them as well, they abandoned their experiment. His lab partner asked him how the early mystics could have learned about emptiness without the aid of a microscope.

One thing we won't be addressing is instances of absolute emptiness in which the relative or full dimension seems absent, which zen refers to as the fallen-away body and mind. Such instances might be refreshing, yet for now we'll confine our exploration to the gentler slopes we're more likely to encounter, and live by, while keeping the backdrop of full-emptiness in our backpack.

Investigating the Five Dimensions of Heartmind

Conventional intellect won't suffice for our inquiry, since we need to discover whether these dimensions of heartmind reside in our very cells. As a short experiment, take several ordinary breaths, feeling the sensations as fully as possible. Notice that within each breath, everything is constantly shifting, never the same for an instant. Are the air in the room and the air in our body really separate, or already merged? The third Zen ancestor, Seng-ts'an, said it this way: "One is no other than all, all no other than one . . . misunderstanding the great mystery, people labor in vain for peace."*

If this sounds confounding, it's good to know that a venerable Zen koan says "Not knowing is most intimate." This unknowableness isn't synonymous with giving up or just not getting it; rather, it's an amazement that emerges as we investigate what's in front of our nose, as well as what's behind it.

If our perplexed monk had had a cheat sheet, he might have understood that the origin of his distress was that he was almost oblivious to the five dimensions, even to the first dimension, physical reality, which was, all the while, sending him blatant messages from every direction.

The path to the unknowing that brings equanimity is through the first four dimensions, in the form of objects, thoughts, emotions, and open spaces. As Soen Roshi, one of my first teachers, used to reiterate, "Each of us *is* this universal, unthinkable, untouchable world."

Let's hypothesize that our mind and body are far from limited to our customary notions, that they are the ideal implements for awakening to what Soen Roshi called "endless dimension, universal life." One event that strengthened my aspiration to awaken to this reality was going with Soen Roshi on New Year's Day to the gravestone of Nyogen Senzaki, an early zen transplant from Japan to America. After grabbing me and several others for a dance on the grass, he put his own monk's robe around the gravestone and held a heartfelt conversation with whatever it was that he perceived. There was a long inscription on the stone, which Soen Roshi

* *The Roaring Stream,* ed. Nelson Foster and Jack Shoemaker (Hopewell, N.J.: Ecco Press, 1996).

translated as: "Always keep your head cool and your feet warm." Or was it heart? Soen Roshi said, "Heart," and laughed.

As we become more acquainted with the five dimensions, awareness of the full-empty dimension can slip in gently, like morning dew trembling on a leaf, falling, falling to earth and quenching the thirst of the seeds of heartmind nestled there. Like walking the morning mist, we may discover at some point that we're wet through and through.

Empty, Yet Full of Mischief?

The paradoxical interplay of the five dimensions of heartmind has confounded zen people at least since the seventh century. Two contenders for sixth Zen ancestor, Hui Neng and the lesser-known Shen Hsiu, competed in a poetry contest, which was supposed to divulge which one of them was ripe to become the successor of their teacher, Hung Jen. Shen Hsiu, a respected member of the monk class, wrote a poem addressing the relative, or phenomenal, side of things, the full aspect of full-emptiness, saying that the mirror, or mind, must be polished through meticulous practice so that it doesn't become clouded by dust or delusion. Hui Neng, an illiterate rice sorter who wasn't permitted in the meditation hall with the monks, had to ask someone to write down his poem for him. He invoked the empty, or absolute, side of the full-empty dimension, saying that in truth there's no dust, no mirror, and therefore nothing to polish. While such a view is a powerful shock to our usual way of seeing things, relative and absolute are two aspects of the same reality, so we don't want to ignore relativity, the attire worn by full-emptiness. Maybe another verse is in order: "No mirror, plenty of dust."

With Shen Hsiu and Hui Neng as role models, we might want to lighten up a little, rather than beat ourselves up for feeling unequal to the path of awakening. The only conclusion that makes sense is to acknowledge that the path of awakening must be ongoing.

And—a Smorgasbord of the Five Dimensions of Heartmind: A Checklist

I've considered getting the five dimensions tattooed on my palm, so they'd be at hand when I was unaware of what was out of my range of awareness.

The word *and*, sometimes dismissed as a mere connective, is useful here; *and*, after all, isn't spiritual practice the ultimate connective?

The first three dimensions, *physical*, *mental*, and *emotional*, are likely to be familiar territory, and the *open awareness* dimension will start to emerge and encompass them as we gain experience with the upcoming meditations and exercises.

No matter how tempting it sounds to go straight for the *full-empty* dimension, heading for the heights before you're familiar with the terrain reminds me of the time my partner, Ezra, and I went up in a hot-air balloon and landed in a tree. The view from the sky was great, but getting out of the tree, with fingers intact, required being rescued—the pilot too.

The "And" checklist exercise uses the definitions of the five dimensions.

And is helpful to raise when awareness seems to have narrowed in a given situation. Global inclusivity can be invited to emerge by checking in on the five dimensions, to see what has gone missing or what is being over-attended.

When confusion arises, run through the dimensions like this: Physical, *and* mental, *and* emotional, *and* open, *and* full-empty. After saying each word, check to see what's present. The word *and* is a reminder to look again. Peek at the book if you don't remember the definitions and contents.

To avoid getting bogged down, move on after spending a few breaths' time on each dimension. A little directed attention with the *and* checklist shines light on all the five dimensions, *and* we'll know which ones are still in the dark.

3 The Seeds of Awakening Heartmind

NURTURING THE FIELD OF INHERENT CAPACITIES

You can tell what Seeds are being watered by noticing what's blooming in your garden.

M. T. HEAD

ONE SUMMER WHILE working on my doctorate, I lived on a farm near the University of Illinois. After torrential rains wiped out the neighboring farmer's tiny cornstalks, he was soon out planting again. As I walked up, he said, "Soybeans." The next month, flooding drowned the new sprouts. Seeing him planting again the following week, I walked over, and he said, "Corn." That's perseverance. It's as essential for

farming as corn and soybeans are, and it is so central to spiritual pı
that it is considered one of the "perfections" in Buddhism, a part o
birthright. Like the other seeds of awakening heartmind, perseveran
already planted; as a desktop icon on my new computer proclaims, "Already installed, activate now."

The seeds of awakening that are already within us range from primarily life-serving ones, like empathy and loving-kindness, to those with the
potential to be life threatening, like anger. Each seed also has a few *ego
hybrids,* which sow discontent. For instance, the seed of equanimity can
hybridize into passivity if the ego heads for the couch to loll in front of the
television for hours rather than doing the things we know are enlivening.
Left unattended, ego hybrids can overrun the very seeds that serve awakening. We're mentioning the hybrids early on, not to sound morose, but
because they're already sprouting.

To come vibrantly alive, the seeds of awakening require cultivation, just
like the seeds in any field. Some respond to the meditations in these pages,
which function similarly to the way a light switch accesses electricity that's
already in the walls.

By the way, seed cultivation doesn't require weed eradication; there's
no need to destroy the ego or the ego hybrids, since both are simply arti-
facts of unclear vision. Attention and use of the practice tools offered here
will naturally compost the ego hybrids into mulch, nourishing the seeds
of wakefulness.

Seeds to Grow By

While all of the seeds of awakening are essential to spiritual practice, the
seeds are grouped by significance and similarities. The first four seeds are

so essential that Buddhism refers to them as *brahma viharas,* or our true home.

1. Compassion. Deep awareness of the suffering of others and oneself. Tolerance and empathy are also signs of this seed. Literally, "embracing suffering (or feeling) altogether, coupled with the wish to relieve it." Ego hybrids: self-pity, insensitivity.

2. Loving-kindness. The "tender mercies" of the Torah's Psalms 17:25 and the New Testament's Philippians 1:8, as well as conventional kindness, benign friendliness, and gentleness. Ego-hybrids: mercilessness, prideful-ness in being seen as kind.

3. Equanimity, ease of being, patience, collectedness. The ability to be satisfied and to abide gracefully in life's ups and downs. The Bible's Philippians (4:7) *peace that passes understanding* reflects this seed, as does Helen Keller's comment "I do not want the peace which passes understanding, but the understanding which brings peace."* Equanimity has plenty of space, even for discomfort. Ego hybrids: sloth, indifference, impatience, resignation, trying to appear to float untouched above adversity.

4. Empathic goodwill, joy, caring, gratitude. The capacity for happiness; the ability to rejoice in peoples' good fortune and well-being. Ego hybrids: jealousy, ingratitude, torment over others' good fortune, *schadenfreude*—a German word meaning pleasure in others' misfortunes.

5. Insight, clear seeing, accurate view. The fruition of learning to attend to the wonder of what's already present and awake to the full-empty nature of existence. Ego hybrids: the hubris of assuming that we're more awake than may be the case.

* Helen Keller, *Light in My Darkness* (Westchester, Pa.: Chrysalis Books, 1960).

6. Aspiration, existential concerns, hope. The still, small voice of our true nature yearning to be revealed. The word *enthusiasm*, literally "the divine within," speaks to the indigenous quality of this yearning. Ego hybrids: spiritual ambition, greed, expecting the path of awakening to confer rewards or the eradication of unwanted conditions.

7. Inspiration. The wick on aspiration's candle. While aspiration, as used here, refers to waking up, inspiration can apply equally to self-interest. Since our preferences vary, inspiration may include the creative arts, nature, or encouragement from those who exemplify the possibility of living in alignment with one's values. Ego hybrids: waiting for the mood to strike; substituting jump starts and excuses for consistent practice.

8. Integrity, conscience, trustworthiness, right action. The ability to remain attuned to what's important and to live accordingly. Ego hybrids: self-righteousness, guilt, shame, shifting our alleged values to match up with what we want at the time.

9. Livelihood, daily activities, unscheduled time. The ability to prioritize our resources and activities to reflect our purported values. Ego hybrids: Tallulah Bankhead: "Do as I say, not as I do."

10. Resolve, perseverance, intention, diligence. The Sanskrit term *virya* encompasses effort, energy, and motivation, attesting to the need for skillful efforts and determination in service to awakening. Ego hybrids: passivity, inertia, addicton to staying busy, and struggling aggressively for spiritual achievements.

11. Willingness, welcoming, hospitality. The ability to receive what life serves up gracefully and consciously, even if it isn't what we had in mind. Ego hybrids: egocentric willfulness (willpower) and its shadow side, *won't power*, or resistance.

12. *Mindfulness (or sense-fullness).* Physically grounded awareness, including an activity and its surroundings. Ego hybrids: over-meticulousness to the point of untimeliness: sometimes during retreats, kitchen workers mistake slow motion for mindfulness and need reminders to pick up the pace, lest lunch become dinner.

13. *Curiosity, inquiring, questioning.* Open interest; the root, *caritas*, like *cure*, attests to the potential healing nature of mindfulness. Ego hybrids: being nosy or easily distracted, distrustful, or suspicious.

14. *Common sense, practicality, discernment.* The ability to determine appropriate action and follow-through. Ego hybrids: poor judgment, "yes-butting," dutiful drudgery (picture *American Gothic*).

15. *Clear thinking, logic, mental objectivity.* The thought processes that help clarify tasks, or the mind itself, including the observer and objective awareness. Ego hybrids: confusing analyzing or philosophizing with spiritual practice or practical application; think-aholic; priding ourselves on "clear thinking."

16. *Generosity, nurturing, service practice.* Functioning on behalf of our larger body, the community of life. Ego hybrids: needing to be needed, staying so busy helping others that we neglect the solitude required for looking into our own hearts.

17. *Intrapersonal awareness, self-awareness.* Socratic "knowing of the self," echoed in Dogen Zenji's injunction to study the self as a precondition for awakening to (as) all existence. Ego hybrids: making things "all about me," using subjective moods as a determinant for our actions.

18. *Environmental awareness, nature intelligence.* A sensory attunement to plants, animals, the environment, and the so-called objects of the five senses. Ego hybrids: seeing nature as more spiritual than other environs, assuming that happiness requires extensive exposure to nature.

19. The five senses. Gates of perception for sensing our connectedness with the environment. Hearing comes here, whereas active listening follows next. Ego hybrids: sense of gluttony, tuning out the sensory world.

20. Listening. The ability to attend actively to outer and inner communications (conversations and thought tracks). Ego hybrids: feigning interest in what someone is saying while mentally plotting a rebuttal.

21. Interpersonal awareness, social skills. A genuine interest in others, as they are, rather than tailored to our template. The capacity for closeness and intimacy. Ego hybrids: people who need people to the extent that the need for time alone is neglected.

22. Communion, harmony, peacemaking, appropriate speech. The ability to facilitate beneficial interactions and communication. Ego hybrids: obstructionist mind-sets or behaviors, malicious or negative communication.

23. Humor, lightness of heart. The ability to lighten up on our judgments of ourselves or the foibles of others. Ego hybrids: sarcasm, trivializing things with false humor.

24. Bodily enlivenment, kinesthetic vitality, chi. The ability to feel the energetic nature of bodily sensation and movement. Ego hybrids: overexercising to try to outrun agitation, depression, lust, or gluttony.

25. Concentration. The ability to achieve a one-pointed focus; the ability to stay put mentally. Ego hybrids: habitually narrowed attention.

The Heart of Vastness: A Meditation

The rhythm of my heart is the birth and death of all that are alive.
THICH NHAT HANH

When it comes to connecting with what's most important, we have to start where we are, as Pema Chödrön says, in her book of the same title. This isn't so easy; we may be convinced that we know the territory, not realizing that every step is into the unknown. It helps to have guides, and few things have been as helpful to me as the Heart of Vastness meditation.

This meditation has three awareness checkpoints: the chest center, an overall sense of the body, and our environmental surroundings. The somatic epicenter of this meditation, the middle of the chest, is replete with the sensations of our heartbeat and breathing. This area includes acupuncture point Conception Vessel 17, which is on the chest midline. This spot has been considered a portal of compassion and vitality in traditions as diverse as Christianity's Prayer of the Heart, the chakra systems, and traditional Chinese medicine, which considers this area to be the dwelling place of both profound joy and grief, as evidenced by intermingling joy and tears. When we are deeply moved, our hand may go to our chest. You can find the spot by feeling around with a few fingertips until discerning a tender or soft spot. Tuning in to this general area of the body is fine as well.

Let's meet the Heart of Vastness now. Take a few deep breaths, feeling them all the way from your nose to your abdomen, to energize the body. Notice how the movements feel like a balloon inflating and deflating on each cycle of breath. Take an occasional deeper breath to refresh attention.

Now let your attention be enticed to expand into an overall sense of your body, including the contact points between the body, the air, and the ground. Feel those areas for several breaths before moving on. Then let your awareness flow out into the space around you in all directions. Bathe for a while in the sea of sounds, loud and soft, near and far.

While maintaining awareness of your body and surroundings, let your attention come to the center of your chest. As if this spot were the small end of a funnel, on an inhale, breathe whatever you sense and feel into the vortex of this spot. Keeping the middle of your chest as your primary touchstone, notice how everything—your body, sounds, and breathing sensations—interconnect with environmental sights and sounds. Then, to finish, rest in this spacious awareness for as long as you like.

If all of this instruction seems daunting, remember that feeling your breathing in the center of your chest is the most important part of the meditation. People report how hard it is to entertain harsh thoughts about themselves or others when their attention rests there. Words like *heartfelt* and *openhearted* might start to hum with aliveness.

If you have ever played the guitar, you'll recognize how similar this area is to the instrument's soundboard (or amplifier), given the intensity of the sensations that percolate and vibrate there. We're getting acquainted with one of the body's key roles, which is to be an instrument of awakening, playing the symphony of existence.

This meditation can begin to infiltrate different arenas of our daily life, in pauses at the coffee machine, for example, or during a bathroom break. One of the best parts of the Heart of Vastness meditation is that it only takes a minute. If our mind claims it can't stay present, that very thought can invite awareness to our chest center, always beating, calling us home. This meditation is accessible to newcomers, yet it can serve anyone. The Heart of Vastness meditation extends a welcome mat, offering tempting tangible evidence that all phenomena depend intimately on everything else, thus unifying scientific and Buddhist cosmologies.

M. T. Head's picture at the front of the book demonstrates the Heart of Vastness checkpoints: The heart with an eye in its center echoes Lakota Medicine Man Chief Archie Fire Lame Deer's saying that we must learn to see with the eye of the heart as well as the eyes in the head—that is, heartmind. The globe in M.T.'s abdomen reminds us that the world is our actual body. The clouds floating through M.T.'s balloon-airhead demonstrate M.T.'s mantra (courtesy of M. T. Head's music guru, Peter Sprague): "Always keep the sky in your head." The infinity sign reminds us of the big picture.

4 *Comprehensive Zen Practice*

APPLIED AWARENESS
IN THE FIVE DIMENSIONS
OF HEARTMIND

The winds of grace are always blowing, but you have to raise the sail.
RAMAKRISHNA

M Y FIRST ZEN SESSHIN (an intensive meditation retreat) was with Soen Roshi in 1975. Participants came from many backgrounds and were mostly practicing concentration, which was the a primary meditation mode brought to the U.S. from Asia. One day at lunch, peanut butter appeared on the menu; someone must have told Soen Roshi that this was an American zen tradition, since our earlier meals were white rice, tea, pickles, and no condiments. Meals were silent, so a fellow at the end of the table was gesticulating, trying to get the peanut butter to come his way. No one noticed, since we were busy concentrating! Finally Soen Roshi bellowed, "How can you talk about seeing the Dharrrrma [the teachings of reality] if you can't see to pass the peanut butter?" This temporarily jolted our myopic view that concentration alone would wake us up; obviously mindfulness, or attention extended to our activities and surroundings, was also necessary. Undeterred, however, were our hopes of enlightenment through concentration, preferably by the end of the week. I spotted no fewer than seven copies of *The Three Pillars of Zen,* an early bestseller by zen teacher Phillip Kapleau, in the women's dorm, several open to the section on enlightenment experiences.

What I had been trying to do at that first retreat was to enlist concentration, a small part of the mental dimension, to penetrate full-emptiness —nothing short of enlightenment! The equivalent in farming would be to hunker down in a small corner of the farm, without watering, tilling, or feeding the soil, and expect a crop.

It was quite a while before I was convinced of the need for a zen practice to extend beyond concentration and be comprehensive.

Being a slow learner, even after seeing that exploration requires both the microscope of concentration and the telescope of open awareness and mindfulness, I reverted periodically to making concentration the whole zen enchilada. Occasional forays into the open awareness of *shikan taza* (just sitting) were undermined by my difficulty in distinguishing spaciousness from spaciness.

Finally, since this obviously wasn't working, I searched through old texts, finding countless lists that confirmed a practice must, indeed, be comprehensive: the ten thises, four thats, and eightfold thoses. If you haven't seen these lists, don't worry; they include just about anything you can think, say, or do. These lists were a partial answer to an often-raised question: if it's all one, why do there have to be so many complications? Can't we just sit, let everything go, just be, and wake up? No. Oneness manifests through differences, which must be addressed specifically if we are to encounter unity that underlies the differences.

It's easy to fall into a "one technique fits all" mentality, since different techniques have been parceled out to various traditions: *vipassana* (a Buddhist meditation practice) incorporates mindfulness, zen goes for concentration and direct insight through koans, some Hindu and Christian groups employ devotional practices, and down the block at the therapist's office emotions and thinking are tools of the trade. Even though some traditions might emphasize particular modalities, words like zen, *vipassana,* and Buddha come from roots pointing to awakening and insight. A comprehensive practice requires us to be aware of all five dimensions of heartmind and to apply tools that relate to them situationally, as needed. For example, washing sharp knives requires attention to the task, while intense emotional upheavals require us to look at our state of mind.

Speaking of emotions, they seem at times to have been neglected in the spiritual armamentarium, possibly based on the notion that emotions and thinking are deluded and will clear up like fog in sunshine if the light dawns. The fallacy of this is easy to spot; just look around! The meditation world is well populated by those of us whose occasional Aha! moments have been rapidly eclipsed by recurring confusion and delusion. Could it be the ego's handiwork behind the tendency to bypass emotional clarification? Like a thief caught with the goods, the ego evades investigation, saying, "Don't look at *me;* look somewhere else— anywhere else!"

People interested in meditation have always showed up with emotional baggage. I had personal confirmation of this during a retreat, when I feared I'd never measure up and started to cry, but not wanting to be seen as a zen failure, I slipped out of the meditation hall. Heading for my luggage, I practically inhaled a whole box of Wheat Thins that I'd brought along "just in case I arrived too late for dinner." Somehow I made it back for the next sitting period, crammed with crackers and recriminations. The very things I'd been trying to outrun had obviously caught up with me. Once the ego suspects it is under scrutiny, resistance is inevitable. It's the same phenomenon as when your taxes are due, and you spend the entire day cleaning the attic. Instead of resorting to crackers, I was going to need to learn how to make sandwiches—with body sensations (the bread) containing my emotional reactions (the filling) supported on a foundation of environmental awareness (the plate). Otherwise a mess is guaranteed.

Comprehensive practice doesn't require a curriculum of formulaic, one-size-fits-all prescriptions. As jazz trumpeter Charlie Parker once said, "First you learn your axe, then you learn your dots. Then you forget about that stuff and you just blow." Yes, we do have to master the mechanics of our craft, yet at some point we have to "forget all that stuff and just blow," letting all five dimensions coalesce into a whole. We take care not to lose sight of what's most important under a pile of techniques.

The entire repertoire presented in these pages is predicated on the foundation of silent, still meditation without input from reading, writing, talking, or music. However, placing a strong emphasis on meditation doesn't mean becoming a junkie who runs to meditate whenever life gets in our face; meditation reveals that there is no hiding place.

Getting into Special States or Blooming
Where You're Planted?

My determination to achieve enlightenment through concentration at that first retreat was predicated on the belief that a new state of mind would heal my old distress. This brings up a perennial issue: are mystical experiences necessary for awakening? This subject can be a quagmire, given the ease with which we fall into spiritual materialism, or attachment to special states.

I went through a phase of seeking special states, once trying something I read about in a book, sitting motionless until the pain of sitting went away. Hours later, the pain did go away, and so did everything else. No self, no nothing. However, my perceptual shift unshifted rapidly, and I couldn't stand up. I had to be carried to the car and driven home. I got an X-ray the next day to be sure I didn't have serious knee damage.

So, instead of trying to dispel endarkenment through enlightening moments, the emphasis here will be on *experiencing*, that is, maintaining a physically grounded awareness of whatever arises, including states of mind.

Comprehensive practice is the medicine of choice when our seemingly unflappable equanimity falls off precipitously in the face of criticism or adversity. It isn't enough to be able to enter deep states (*samadhi*) during meditation, if we walk into walls because we've misplaced mindfulness. And there's a high price to pay if we're mindful of teacups but unmindful of people—the price of broken relationships, lost livelihood, and eventual isolation.

Comprehensive Practice: A Braid Analogy

When we lose track of the *now, vow, how,* and *bow* that keep the way of awakening comprehensive, we might envision four interweaving strands of a braid. The strands, which form the contents of this book, form a whole that includes, but isn't limited to, the following:

- *Now* means activating open awareness.
- *Vow* means remembering what's most important, starting with awakening wholeheartedly to what life really is and living in accord with our interconnectedness in each moment.
- *Bow* means cultivating the seeds of awakening heartmind to activate our innate capacity for gratitude and the ability to appreciate anything—perhaps even everything
- *How* means having a blueprint for a comprehensive practice, grounded in the five dimensions of heartmind.

All of this may sound complicated, but the purpose is to actualize the capacity to just be. At that first sesshin with Soen Roshi, he seemed, to my admiring, novice eyes, to emanate the quality of just being. One day, when a large number of people who weren't enrolled in the retreat showed up to hear his daily talk, he smiled and said, "Too precious to talk; let's sit." Then he concluded the sesshin by playing a scratchy recording of Beethoven's Ninth Symphony on a child's record player. To my "professional musician" mentality, it was a revelation to watch him relish the music, unimpeded by its acoustic shortcomings.

As we encounter those who demonstrate the possibility of living with such apparent freedom, we can appreciate, one of Soen Roshi's favorite phrases: "Endless dimension, universal life."

Aspiration, Accountability, and Amnesia

Therapists sometimes joke that after fifteen years of therapy some clients can explain eloquently why they're still as stuck as ever. This can also happen in spiritual venues.

If we thought we were through with the education model when we graduated from intellectual and emotional concerns to spiritual aspirations, we may underestimate the importance of accountability. Homework, or life work, is as valuable in the halls of meditation as it is in the halls of ivy. Yet sometimes in the areas we claim to consider most important, like living wakefully and heartfully, we may let accountability slide. If we treated our teeth or cars the way we treat (or mistreat) the essentials of our being, the consequences would be obvious.

Meditation is our primary spiritual homework, and it can be supplemented with other activities and exercises to increase accountability.

It sounds straightforward, doesn't it? Apiration, accountability. What's the catch? Amnesia. We forget. And forget. And forget. When amnesia strikes in the domain of what we hold to be most important, we may not recognize that it has taken charge, given that amnesia's very nature is forgetfulness. We might forget about practice altogether for a while, or spend meditation periods lost in reverie or problem solving; I once planned a whole college course during a retreat. If we meditate for an hour or a half-hour in the morning, and perhaps in the evening, followed by twenty-some hours in a state of waking or dozing sleep, those aren't good odds for waking up.

Amnesia likes to rationalize, saying that we're often too busy to keep our zen practice commitments. However, since practice is a code word for applied awareness, whatever is keeping us busy, such as working at a computer or teaching a class, qualifies as a time for practice. It usually takes a while before we discover that starting the day with meditation has a funny way of seeming to add time to our day.

Amnesia likes to confuse terms like *awake* and *aware*. We'll have to use these on a sliding scale, ranging from finite to infinite. *Awakening* and *awareness* interweave, since without awareness, we're practically asleep on our feet. While *awake* can imply increasing awareness across the five dimensions, that's probably not the case very often. Likewise, *awareness* doesn't necessarily imply transformation, and even moments of awakened perception don't necessarily enhance awareness. Zen adepts can be mindless drivers, while top-ranked athletes with 360-degree awareness don't necessarily demonstrate compassion and insight, the fruits of living with increasing wakefulness. Obviously, these terms need to be used judiciously so we don't end up reinforcing amnesia.

Amnesia and aspiration are so central to spirituality that they are cited at least as far back as the fifth-century Tibetan Abidharma, the earliest psychospiritual system still in use to my knowledge. Among other things, it describes mental factors that foster aspiration, including compassion, clarity, generosity of spirit, beneficial action, and the ability to be satisfied. The shadow side of aspiration consists of the obstructing mental factors that we're calling amnesia: opinionatedness, indecisiveness, arrogance, anger, neediness, jealousy, gloominess, worry, laziness, and forgetfulness—the quintessential amnesia. Such factors can help pinpoint areas where homework might provide accountability and encourage aspiration.

You can even enlist the ego in the process, as I did when I originally moved to a zen center; I knew that living there would get me out of bed for dawn meditation, since I didn't want to look like a slacker to the other residents. Something deeper was at work too—aspiration. Obviously, this approach has limitations in the absence of consciousness-boosting activities, otherwise organizations that pride themselves on discipline would have the most awake participants.

To review, aspiration reminds us of what's most important; accountability provides ways to clarify and actualize the process; and even amnesia can be of value as we start to recognize our particular versions of it.

A mainstay of ZCSD's daily schedule is the reciting of the "Practice Principles," reminders of both amnesia and aspiration. Eloquently crafted by ZCSD member Allan Kaprow, the first two lines express the pull of amnesia: "Caught in the self-centered dream (or dream of self), only suffering; / Holding to self-centered thoughts, exactly the dream." The last two lines reflect our aspiration to remember what's most important: "Each moment, life as it is, the only teacher; / Being just this moment, compassion's way." The second couplet is more likely to remain central, if we understand the need for accountability to help bolster our aspiration. Even when amnesia is singing its siren song, if we listen deeply, we may hear the murmur of heartmind, whispering quietly.

WIPITS: What Is Practice in This Situation?
A Worksheet

For accountability in keeping aspiration and amnesia sorted out, WIPITS, or "what is practice in this situation?" is advisable.

Often awareness is scant in at least one area. The WIPITS categories cover the main modes of human perception and functioning. Even if the full-empty dimension sounds like pea soup for now, let's keep it on the table so that it will be fit for consumption when the time is ripe.

Each dimension of heartmind includes a brief description, followed by suggestions for how to hone awareness in each area.

1. *Physical dimension.* This is the who, what, where, and when—the location, situation, people, things, action, and sensory phenomena involved in the situation. Hone awareness of this dimension by feeling the body's sensations and movements; tune in the sounds, sights, smells, and the sense objects that are the stuff of life.

2. *Mental dimension.* This is our thoughts relating to a situation. Hone awareness of this dimension by knowing what thoughts are passing through.

3. *Emotional dimension.* This is the mood or emotional tone we hold, in general or as a reaction to a situation. Hone awareness of this dimension by seeing if you can differentiate the various components of an emotion—the thoughts, bodily sensations, sense of self, and the intensity that characterizes emotions. Is there a word that describes your emotion or mood?

4. Open awareness dimension. This is the environmental spaciousness that enmeshes the situation, the inclusivity of the moment. Hone awareness of this dimension by letting the sounds and spaciousness of the environment invite the senses to open in all directions.

5. Full-empty dimension. Here we encounter the wonder at the heart of things, even if it's primarily an intellectual intimation at first. When all of the descriptions and intellectual concepts concerning these dimensions fall away, what remains? A shorthand version of WIPITS is:

- What's going on?
- What am I adding?
- What am I leaving out?
- What do I truly know?

5 *The Body*

IDENTITY, OR INSTRUMENT OF AWAKENING?

All of you who wish to plumb this deep source must make the investigation in secret with your entire body.

HAKUIN EKAKU ZENJI

THE PHYSICAL DIMENSION of heartmind spans a monumental spectrum, from bodily sensations to sensory input. The senses are our main mode of perception, antennae that experience physical phenomena in our environment. With the physical dimension, we already have signs that no dimension exists alone, a portent of the inseparability of all five dimensions: where is there any demarcation line that separates hearing, what is heard, and the air?

The reason we look into the five dimensions individually is that by investigating their aggregates (*skandhas*), which constitute all of our living experience, using the stuff of our own body as our research tools, we are better able to fathom the whole of reality.

Looking into the physical dimension, we find that thinking is so endemic to humans that it will do its best to usurp the evidence provided by the five senses. You can see this in the academic realm, where, until recently, the emphasis has been almost exclusively on mathematics and other symbolic systems as the primary learning modes, without recognizing the value of the myriad intelligences that Harvard's Dr. Howard Gardner recognized in his seminal work on multiple intelligences. His inclusion of the musical, kinesthetic, and spatial (physical) intelligences, key components of our birthright of capabilities, is much appreciated by musicians and athletes, who still find that their subjects are regularly considered "frills" in academia.*

As a result of this overly mental orientation, most of us believe we have to think our way through situations. We're left hard-pressed to experience the fullness of life sensorially, or even to use language effectively to communicate in areas that aren't bounded by thinking, which includes a great deal of what we hold to be most important.

I went through a phase of using nondual language as a training tool, minimizing "I, me, my" language to deconstruct the ego. But the main effect it had, even though it did slow down the speed of self-centered thinking, was to irritate people. I didn't sound as awake as I had hoped,

* Howard Gardner, *Changing Minds* (Cambridge, Mass.: Harvard Business School Press, 2004).

and it added a certain disembodied tone to my talks and writings; as you may have noticed, not all traces of this tendency have been eradicated.

Since we so often overlook the somatic nature that embeds our mental and emotional activity, we may think we know more about physicality than we do. I found this out when I started zen practice, having presumed after years of music making, dancing, and all the other physical facts of life, that I was well acquainted with the parameters of physicality. Apparently not. About the same time, I took up African and Brazilian drumming and dance. The merger of meditation, music, and dance reduced to rubble the walls I had constructed between disciplines; Brazilian Carnaval was the final jolt, when immersion in the vibratory force of hundreds of drummers shattered old personal and musical boundaries into wholeness.

My pet theories also took some strong hits. My sabbatical research project, on the need to unify mind and body, was obsolete, as felt evidence confirmed that you don't have to connect things that aren't separate to begin with. A simple headache should have made it obvious to me that brains are body parts.

Science is also nibbling away at the thinking plague, displacing the head, or brain actually, from its assumed supremacy in all things. Research in so-called heart intelligences is on the upsurge, joining the meditation world's long-standing interest in this area.

Meditation gobbled up my former divisions of life: into meditation and nonmeditation, spiritual and secular. Our days of hoping things will stay neatly in their old categories are numbered. Once we commence zen practice, our mind and body, physical and mental functions, along with all the others, must venture into the unknown.

The Body

Our first stop in the physical dimension is the body, our oldest and best acquaintance. Since it has been around so long, we may think we know it well. Yet it holds unrealized talents that are ideal for unlocking our mental doors and revealing how the five dimensions commune intimately, making connections we may not have suspected, just as our physical and mental functions conspire together to read these words.

Spiritual traditions view the body the same way many individuals do—as bad news. After all, spiritual groups are composed of people, and how many people have you met who don't have an adversarial relationship with their body? The bad press for the body goes back at least as far as the earliest spiritual communities, with their countless regulations for keeping bodies under wraps and free from temptation by other interesting, or interested, bodies. Attitudes toward the body, then as now, range from seeing it as an outright enemy to declaring it prime property for a self-improvement project. During his zealous phase, Saint Francis referred to his body as "Poor Brother Ass," seeing it as a pesky inconvenience that was unavoidably necessary for getting around. How many of us likewise deduced in our Sunday school days that *body* and *evil* are sin-onyms, just like sin and sex? As Saint Francis matured, he seems to have reasoned that the mind takes the body for a ride more often than vice versa. He then began calling his body "My Dear Ass," a somewhat more cordial relationship.

One of the more intriguing non sequiturs we manage to entertain is the notion that the "self" is somehow external to our body. This dubious notion typifies a favorite ego strategy: cooking up mischief and assigning the blame elsewhere, sort of like shooting someone and then blaming the gun. We can even manage the consummate cognitive dissonance of regarding our body simultaneously as both self and other: "I'm not the body; I'm nothing but the body." James Joyce describes this artfully in *The Dubliners*: "Mr. Duffy lived at a short distance from his body, regarding his own acts with doubtful side-glances."

Then there are classic religious phrases disowning the body and sounding like projection or ventriloquism: "The devil made me do it"; "The spirit is willing, but the flesh is weak."

With all of this negativity and disowning of the body, it's a blast of fresh air to meet broader perspectives, like a morning salutation I learned from Cherokee elders: "Getting up in the morning, I put on my real body, the world." Then consider Japanese Zen ancestors like Chao Chou (Joshu in Japanese) and Hakuin, with their reminders that our body is the very body of the Awakened One (the Buddha, reality).*

Sadly, yet not surprisingly, zen practitioners can hear these lines repeatedly without considering how starkly they contrast to the aversion we hold for the body we take everywhere.

Our disaffection is so ingrained that even following glimpses of the wondrous nature of all things, including our body, all it takes is an advertisement or a comment to spark self-consciousness about our anatomical proportions, and the me-versus-my-body dichotomy springs up again, hydralike.

We weren't always like this. If you have baby pictures, take them out and behold the uninhibited, unselfconscious abandon they demonstrate. There

* Hakuin, *Song of Zazen,* Zen Center San Diego Service Book.

we were, attired in the unfettered posture of a baby learning to walk—upright, head afloat, torso inflated—check us out! Then, *foomp*—we plopped to earth, shed a few tears, and were off to the next adventure. Enter toddlerhood, with its necessary societal conditioning. There's no way to avoid teaching children not to run into the street unattended, and probably few, if any, cultures encourage sleeping, eating, and excreting exactly when the body calls. So before long we start tuning out physical signals, around the time we're being taught the difference between using our diapers and using the toilet. Missed cues and painful encounters with stairs, swings, streets, siblings, parents, and other kids lead us to unpleasant conclusions about our body and the fact that it can be hurt. Then we receive so-called constructive criticism about our body's positions and by-products: "Stand up straight!" "Suck in that gut!" "Don't touch!" "Was that *you*?"

Eventually we find ourselves insulated in a mishmash of attitudes that bespeak bodily denigration. There's an observable diminution in learning rate as children move toward puberty, sometimes attributed to the fact that the neural pathways become less flexible. However, that can't be the whole story of slowed learning, since the cerebral cortex is simultaneously developing, suggesting that children would learn faster as they go. Could it be that rapidity of learning is impacted by increased inhibition, self-consciousness, and fear of failure? I'm no brain scientist, but after forty years of teaching all age levels, this phenomenon of learning slowdown has always fascinated me. Rarely do you see toddlers agonizing over making mistakes, yet as children move through primary school, you see them trying to avoid looking foolish. It takes tremendous brainpower to construct an image and keep it intact. How much energy can remain for learning and staying open to what life offers?

Before our first decade closes, our attention is shifting from exploring life at large to looking as acceptable as possible, at least to our peer group. Take the difference in relating to pain: small children scream when they're hurt, while older ones try to look unbothered by minor to moderate pain. Physical awareness diminishes through inattention, and as adults we can attest to the results of ignoring a muscle or tendon that's shouting, "Please! Stop. *Now.*"

Disowning bodily awareness is nothing new. Centuries ago, a middle-aged monk asked Chao Chou what zen was all about, and he said, "When you're tired, sleep; when you're hungry, eat." The irate monk rebutted that any child of seven knew that, whereupon Chao Chou responded that he hadn't noticed any monks of sixty doing it. By adulthood, when someone asks if we're hungry, we look at our watch! Stephen Levine, meditation teacher and author, tells of hungry stomachs that head to the kitchen for salad and are distracted on the way by a box of candy. Five pieces of candy later, the same mind that stopped for candy sneers, "Haven't you got any self-control?" There are no winners in this civil war between the Disunited States of Mind.

Eventually our body's capacity to sense and feel is overridden by its function as an appliance or a clotheshorse, serving the ego. If we pride ourselves on our intelligence, we may regard our body as a think tank, like a Silicon Valley corporation intended to crank out good ideas.

As we worship at the shrine of bodily contempt, our credo comes to resemble an advertisement: "May the latest product fix this unacceptable body." If our ego finds the body an unacceptable abode, where are we expecting to find more favorable environs?

Unlearning Conditioned Bodily Responses

The body is a sensing instrument, equipped with a central receiving and perceiving capacity. So let's start with feeling, physically, the bodily posture we maintain: does it reflect a skewed stance toward life? On all sides we see bodily dispositions—or rather indispositions, given their contortions and tight musculature. Collapsed torsos seem to broadcast low self-esteem: "They probably see how hopeless I am, so I'll try to be invisible." Then we have the defensive "You can't make me" pose; walking demonstrations of frustration; the cringe of French sculptor Auguste Rodin's *Thinker*; and puffed-up facades of power, possibly covering something quite the opposite.

Postures don't always imply the presence of particular mental or emotional states, yet every actor knows the extent to which they can be psychological gestures. Try slumping over, with eyes downcast, and see what thought immediately comes to mind. Then assume a jauntily erect stance and see what your mind says. They're not called posturings for nothing. Whether we look tight, inflated, or as collapsed as a dog capitulating in a territorial battle, we're usually more tense or slack than just getting around requires.

We might even feel undressed if our habitual kinesthetic kinks aren't locked in place, as I found during my early sitting days when the monitors would come by and correct my posture. I had no idea that my body listed to the left, after years of adapting to a leg shortened by childhood polio. Why, I wondered, did they keep adjusting me into what seemed like a crooked position? Within minutes of being corrected, familiar off-balance tensions would reflexively pull me sideways again, and with relief I'd think, "Ahhh! Straight again. That's more like it." Or you might be dancing with abandon, and a sudden thought of your self-image flips your delicious relaxation into a cringe of self-conscious shame.

Probably the phrase "Why don't you just relax" should be a misdemeanor; we would if we could. A bodyworker once told me that as long as there were zen students, he'd make a good living! Photos from my early meditation years provide evidence of this, as I diligently emulated photos from zen books (which turned out to be mostly of statues). Shoulders in my earlobes, hands squeezed together, I looked as if I were trying to keep from falling apart.

This is too powerful to go on forever. When the time comes that we're ready to call off the battle with our body, here are some tools that might be of use:

- Delete possessive pronouns periodically, replacing the phrase "my body" with "this body"—but not aloud. You may be surprised to discover how much tension accompanies the notions of ownership and doer-ship that this language reflects.
- Give names to your habitual demeanors, both the physical ones and the mental ones that influence them: one of mine is "Miss Demeanor." The simple act of giving a name to predictable negative thoughts about the body increases our awareness of bodily behaviors considerably. If we don't catch those twisting thoughts as they arise, they will turn into wrenches, literally torquing tendons that are already overly tight. Two other dramatis personae that I can count on for regular appearances are the supercilious Hortensia, who punctuates her pompous pontifications with a wagging index finger, and Sister Basilica, who thinks she's quite spiritual, doesn't look where she's going,

and steps in potholes. She's not interested in cracking the koan "Pride goeth before a fall." Using language like this isn't intended as reprogramming but as a way to bring attention to programming that is already running.

- *Stop* periodically to feel your bodily posture for several breaths.
- Adopt a balanced, flexible position—whether standing, sitting, or lying. Then feel how rapidly the familiar postural quirks reassert themselves. Can you hear the voice of the Godfather? "Just when I thought I was out, they [the kinks] keep pulling me back in."

As our bodily sensations become more familiar territory, the long-standing rebar that held our bodies in their old positions turns out, we find, to be less solid than it had seemed. There's probably no better firsthand evidence of impermanence than noticing our own bodily sensations. As they shift, moment by moment, we can feel their somatic sheath blending into the sensory cascade of the moment.

Bodily awareness gets us in touch with some important data: bodies feel. They move. They digest, breathe, vibrate, and sing. And as with any instrument, appropriate usage supports optimal functioning. Like a Stradivarius violin found in someone's attic, the body's natural capacities need regular tune-ups in order to shine forth. And the finest harpsichord deteriorates unless caring hands evoke its song.

It may be a while before long-standing notions of the body-as-our-sole-identity are dismantled and replaced by firsthand knowledge that the body functions as a representative and perceiver of the five dimensions of heartmind and universal reality. It is the optimal instrument for awakening to them. If this sounds grandiose, isn't it much more so to claim that these amazing capacities are owned by our personal self?

Over time, as our body acquires dents and develops malfunctions, we'll be happy to discover empirical confirmation that our actual identity is far more inclusive than we've admitted and is intimately interconnected to other people, the earth, and the air—an inseparable whole, a formless field.

Breathing — Head, Heart, and Hara

Breathing is the body function most identified with many spiritual traditions; just look at how rich spiritual vocabulary is in breath-related words: *inspiration, aspiration, pneuma,* and *spirituality* itself. Still, if our life depended on being aware of our breathing, most of us would be dead. The unawareness that we extend to breathing is a microcosm of the general lack of attention we pay to much of life. Fortunately for our survival, breathing is part of the autonomic nervous system and keeps on rolling, like Ol' Man River, even if we're preoccupied with things that aren't happening.

Breathing methods are among the best-known physiologically grounding practices. These include counting or holding the breath, breathing with sounds, and focusing on the breath in areas of the body. Breathing techniques are sometimes localized in the head, heart, or *hara,* the Japanese term for the lower abdomen that has entered the spiritual and martial arts vocabularies. Being aware of our breathing in the head and nostrils is useful in developing generic body awareness and concentration and for maximizing wakefulness when sleepiness strikes. Breathing centered in the chest or heart area is sometimes associated with particular seeds of awakening and is featured in the Heart of Vastness and Loving-Kindness meditations. Abdominal, *hara,* breathing is particularly popular for developing power, stability, and energy, making it the breath of choice for many physical exercises and enterprises, and useful in working with anger.

It's usually preferable not to try to change something, like breathing, until we have experienced it as it is *now*. Unaltered, unadorned breathing is the basic approach advocated here for general meditation.

Sometimes when we attend to the utter simplicity of breathing, the ego is left feeling unemployed. So there's a temptation to turn breathing into a project by making it longer, deeper, slower, smoother—hounding the breath as if it were a dog on a leash. Attempts to manipulate the breath usually manage to foul it up, as I learned from childhood asthma. Stage fright also impacts breathing powerfully, a fact well known to public speakers, singers, and wind instrument players. If a musician's breathing is erratic, it will be hard to breathe life into the phrasing of a melody, and the performance will be literally uninspiring—a testament to the connection of breathing and states of mind.

When emotions are strong, people sometimes hyperventilate, hold their breath, pant, or barely breathe. These are instances of how a frightened mind fails to differentiate between what is actually life threatening and *perceived* threats to our self-image. As a result, emotional reactions can be as dangerous to our well-being as the situations that provoke the reaction. Even without a gun, the ego can kill.

Why not invite the little mind and heartmind to conspire, literally—that is, to breathe together—and get to know the breath intimately? Experiencing breathing, just as it is, provides tastes of the non-doing and letting-be that permeate zen teachings. The breath is a gracious escort, welcoming awareness back when it has departed. No exertion is necessary, only awareness; breathing doesn't require winding up or plugging anything in. It's a present; in fact it *is* the present. When our attention focuses on the breath stream for even a few moments, we find a living testament to life's unity, a marvel that extends from our first inbreath, or inspiration, to our final expiration. Take a moment right now to feel and sense the breath stream, and see if you find any boundaries.

6 *Still, Silent Sitting*

A MEDITATION ON THE FIVE
DIMENSIONS OF HEARTMIND

The speedy route to clear seeing? Try the five Ss: Sitting, Stillness,
Silence, Solitude, and Staying Put.

M. T. HEAD

STILL, SILENT SITTING meditation forms a common thread
in many spiritual traditions and assumes a place of centrality in zen,
which has always viewed sitting as essential to the awakening of heartmind. In fact, the Japanese term for seated meditation is *zazen*, "sitting
zen." One of the innumerable paradoxes that dot the zen landscape is that
sitting still and doing nothing is considered a key component in the awakening of our essential nature.

If sitting as described here is difficult or impossible for you for health reasons, don't worry. The word *sitting* refers to far more than a bodily position; while physical balance and stability are valuable, the bodily position isn't nearly as important as the sense of presence that pervades us. Books, videos, and meditation venues can demonstrate postures conducive to still, silent meditation, using a cushion, chair, or bench. There's nothing intrinsically noble about sitting still, silent, and erect, although these attributes are often depicted as expressions of our inherent dignity and wholeness.

Paradoxically, sitting in silent solitude, consciously and openly, can highlight the store of distress that regularly brings people to meditation. The occasional leg pain we might experience during meditation is minor in comparison with the discomfort our mind cooks up, often almost unnoticed—that is, until we sit in still silence. The ways we squirm—physically, mentally, and emotionally—come out of hiding, which, we may be surprised to find, is a significant part of the winding road to equanimity.

The length of sitting periods varies, with thirty minutes being common. It's better to attempt what's possible and practical rather than pursue potentially discouraging ideals. The following sitting tune-up is a variant on zen's *shikan taza,* with specific checkpoints for accountability in maintaining broad-spectrum awareness.

Sitting Tune-Up: Guided Meditation

The italicized words in the descriptions below can serve as physically based reminders of things to *sense* and *feel* during sitting periods. They will be numbered for now, as a suggested order during the learning process. Most of the items refer to the physical components of sitting, and a few mention upcoming topics like concentration, breath counting, and dealing with thoughts, to keep the lens of awareness focused.

1. *Sitting down.* As you sit down, feel the sensations of your weight shifting from your feet to your seat. Let the weight become evenly distributed and erect on a *tripod base* formed by the bottom of your spine and both knees or feet.

2. *Balance and alignment.* Give your body weight to the floor. Let your head and torso float skyward, as if your head contained a helium-filled balloon. Encouraging your weight to *sink* earthward as the torso *floats* skyward helps you to come into alignment with gravity and permits the body to lengthen and soften into a resourceful and receptive position.

3. *Infinitesimal sway.* Periodically feel the body's *invisible fluctuation,* like underwater seaweed, with its tentacles rooted to the ocean floor and its branches swaying freely with the currents. Awareness of this subtle sway counterbalances rigidity and long-held contortions. Even skyscrapers sway imperceptibly.

4. *Head and eyes.* Keep your eyes slightly lowered, at about a forty-five-degree angle, with a comfortable, unfocused gaze, as if *seeing through* the world rather than looking at anything in particular. Take care that your head stays erect, an extension of your spine. Your chin is neither tucked in nor jutting out, both of which increase the tendency toward sleep or rumination.

5. *Hands.* Your hands remain folded in your lap or resting on your legs.

6. *Breathing.* Breathe naturally and quietly through your nose, feeling the torso *inflating* and *deflating,* like an airbag or an accordion. Con-

sider phrases like *air in the body*, or breathing, and *body in the air*, or posture, to help refresh awareness of your breathing, your physical position, and the omnipresence of air. Periodically, feel your breath stream as it moves within you and merges with the air in the room, bringing awareness to the interweaving of body and environment.

7. *Concentration.* To start a meditation period, you might count your breaths to focus attention, numbering your exhales from one to ten to keep awareness on track.

8. *Thought labeling.* If any of your frequent flyer thoughts are eager to co-opt your attention, notice them and then echo them back verbatim, as if a parrot were sitting on your shoulder, preceding the thought with the word *thinking*.

9. *Strongest physical sensation.* For a few rounds of breathing, feel your most intense bodily sensations, without trying to change them.

10. *Surround sound.* As your awareness opens, include environmental sounds and sense the encompassing airspace.

11. *Flickering.* Let your attention flicker between bodily sensations and sensory awareness.

12. *Letting-be.* At this point, all of the above is included within awareness, without focusing on any one thing. This inclusive, open awareness is the portal to the five dimensions of heartmind, a primary step into a slowly dawning awareness that as we're unfolding into the moment, we're simultaneously enfolded by it. This is the letting-be so dear to the heart of zen.

13. *Prioritizing physicality.* Since physical awareness is more tangibly real than our head trips, it's the preferred focus of sitting.

14. *When all else fails, follow instructions!* The old mind can't be expected to have much interest in the simplicity of being. If a

thought storm occurs, a brief return to thought labeling can bring some lucidity.

The only place we're trying to get to is right here. It's tempting to skip the parts that sound boring or difficult, but they prove to be quite tasty if we keep nibbling at them.

15. *Accountability checkpoints.* When your attention strays, consult the italicized words and numbered headings above for pointers. These are essentials that need to be included within awareness, for accountability when amnesia sets in.

16. *Remembering what's important.* It's easy to get lost in the mechanics of sitting techniques and forget the point: activating the seeds of awakening and the five dimensions of heartmind.

17. *Knowing what we're up to.* After trying sitting for a while, ask yourself whether you could describe the process to someone else. That's one of the best ways of seeing whether or not we know what we're up to. Sometimes diagramming what goes on increases our objective awareness of both the process and what is added by our personal agendas. You might also consider what your response would be if someone asked you why you were engaged in meditation practice.

18. *Practice consultation.* Conferring with a zen practice consultant or teacher can be useful, if one is available.

7 Mindfulness in Activity

Mystical power and wondrous activity: carrying water and chopping firewood.

LAYMAN PANG

MINDFULNESS COULD ALSO be referred to as "sense-full-ness," since it includes the body, the senses, the environment—indeed the all-encompassing embrace of open awareness. On our trips to Australia, Ezra and I have enjoyed signs in ferryboats and trains saying Mind Your Head (or Step), and Dispose of Trash Thoughtfully. That's mindfulness.

We might wonder why mindfulness needs to be developed; after all, hasn't life always consisted of one activity after another? It's because we have also developed the ability to be almost oblivious to, or at least distracted from, whatever tasks we're in the middle of.

One of the major things that lead to lost consciousness, or a lack of attention, is our litany of expectations. A major proponent of thwarting expectations, Allan Kaprow, a longtime member of the zen center of San Diego, developed the "Happening" with John Cage back in the fifties. A Happening involves whatever is happening in a given setting, and Allan graciously offered to sponsor one during the zen center's early days on Black Mountain (outside San Diego). As people arrived, they were handed brooms or rakes, and they began tidying the grounds enthusiastically, anticipating an imminent performance. Soon enthusiasm waned, yielding to outright irritation in a few cases: *where was the Happening?* Allan announced with delight, "This *is* the Happening!" Not everyone was delighted. "Life as art" may sound great—until it undresses our repertoire of requirements concerning what constitutes art. Or life.

Expectations aren't the only impediment to mindfulness; what about daydreaming and boredom? Since these diversions amplify mindlessness, our early attempts at mindfulness may be as awkward as learning to ride a bike: homing in on a small part of the action, we lose sight of the rest and fall flat on our face. The first time I engaged in mindful walking at a meditation retreat, I couldn't imagine how I had ever learned to walk. Eventually we discover that our eyes, feet, and thoughts actually inhabit the same location. But until then, we'll understand why M. T. Head says, "Mindlessness leads to groundlessness."

Take, for instance, mindful driving. Considering the way we drive, it's a miracle that we're alive. Once I drove Rosa Parks into Canada to meet a busload of kids at the end of the Underground Railroad, and I ran a stop sign before figuring out the logic behind their locations in that country. She launched into a spirited lecture on mindfulness: "Elizabeth, don't you teach mindfulness? Mindfulness is very important in driving; it can save your life." Her comments upped my driving awareness radically.

If we have become more adept at chopping up life than the chopping wood of zen koan fame, then it may take a while before we discover the marvelous activity inherent in things we have considered boring. If years of being unsatisfied have turned us into dissatisfaction factories, it will take some intentional mindfulness to reactivate the freshness and curiosity that can make almost everything interesting. When I visited Allan Kaprow shortly before his death in March 2006, with eyes shining he said, "When you really pay attention to something, it turns out that everything is interesting." If it's not clear what mindfulness entails in a particular situation, ask, "What's the primary movement, or activity, right now?" That's where awareness belongs. Mindfulness helps us realize that the current activity, like it or not, is the very moment that we've been looking for.

Moving Meditation and Systems: The Care and Feeding of Our Animal

Moving meditation, like most meditative approaches, is primarily a path of liberation. It has been part of the spiritual curriculum for millennia, traversing a spectrum from slow forms like chi kung (or energy cultivation) and yoga to the speedy flash of kung fu. The interpenetrating nature of stillness and action, body and universe, is alluded to in some zen koans, and it can be experienced viscerally through moving meditation.

Zen folklore and Taoist and martial arts sources concur that when Zen founder Bodhidharma reached China's Shaolin Monastery in the sixth century, he found the monastics physically and mentally listless.

Their daily routine apparently consisted of quietistic meditation and treatise study. According to legend, Bodhidharma headed for a cave and meditated for nine years, contemplating ways to light their fire. At least one part of this legend has to be apocryphal—the part about his legs falling off from all that meditation. This part of the story can't be true if Bodhidharma not only introduced chi kung into the monastic regimen but is also credited with creating kung fu, to allow awareness to attain top speed.

Bodhidharma deserves the nickname Body-dharma, in light of his emphasis on physically active meditation. In a koan, he told his students that one had attained his skin, one his flesh, another his bone, but that only one had attained his marrow. Considering his emphasis on kinesthetic meditation forms, even if this story is only metaphorical, it reminds us of the importance of penetrating to the bone, to the marrow, of life.

Fast-forwarding to the eighteenth century, Hakuin, Japan's best-known Zen teacher of the day, also developed a movement meditation series. Parts of it are included in ZCSD's Mindful Movement series (along with some of Bodhidharma's "Hand of Awakening" chi kung series and some traditional Chinese meridian chi kung movements). A few of the movements are ones I learned from the Nipponzan Myohoji Buddhist monks, who were walking across the U.S. to establish a Peace Pagoda. I didn't walk very far with them, but periodically everyone would stop walking and do a little chi kung to revitalize flagging energy.

Moving meditation can help us *feel* the chi as its animating force freely traverses the body. We may have some trouble sensing it, even during moving meditation, if tight muscles have enchained our cells, leaving us feeling burdened, as if Greek mythology's Sisyphus and his boulder were in our shoulder.

My active involvement with mindful movement, as part of zen training, began at a sesshin with Soen Roshi. Outside every morning at 3:00 A.M., after some *dharma dancing,* or free-form movements on the grass, we did specific movements accompanied by the words "All is revealed as it is—nowwwww." I was confused; if everything is already revealed, why in the world are we meditating twelve hours a day, sleeping four, and getting up hours before dawn to do movements in the middle of a gang-boundary street? (One participant was arrested after telling a policeman not to touch him because he was meditating.)

I didn't realize at first that what made things seem so strenuous was in large part my tightly wound condition. After all, Soen Roshi didn't seem to be struggling at all. When the moving mind isn't obliterating awareness of the chi, we sense the purring, flowing, wave-and-particle nature of the body.

This brings us to the issue of movement systems, and other forms of meditation, being touted for their potential health benefits. While many forms of chi kung and yoga may have such effects, we need to keep in mind our deepest wish: awakening to the interconnectedness of health and illness and to the ability to function harmoniously with whatever life presents. Neither experiencing chi nor being in the zone is synonymous with being awake. Even if seductive bliss occurs, it can't override the physical, mental, and emotional conditioning that are guaranteed to be waiting in the wings when our endorphins slump. It's nice to be as healthy as possible, yet we reinforce dualistic, separating notions when we become preoccupied with outrunning adversity and hoping to die in perfect health.

Always, what's most important is to remain mindful, focused on the activity at hand. Jet Li, a world-class mindful-movement luminary, expressed this recently on his website: "The only way to be truly liberated is if you learn to care about others, to give love and compassion."[*]

World Body: A Walking Meditation

How rarely we notice the earth, much less have any gratitude for its presence. We walk all over it, rarely recognizing it as our very body, our life itself.

The term *world body* refers to the understanding reflected in this quote from Chögyam Trungpa Rinpoche: "The whole world is your body. There's a tendency to view the body as your private possession. And because of that, you tend to forget the rest of the world and the greater orbit of experience involved with that. If a person is able to relate with the world, he is also able to relate with the body."[†]

After some experience with silent, still, seated meditation, mindfulness can extend into walking, preferably starting with the walking periods that are interspersed between seated meditation periods. Actually, walking anywhere is fine; however, the slow pace recommended here might attract undesirable attention on Fifth Avenue, or when your boss has just told you to rush an assignment.

Before starting, stand still for a few breaths. Feel your body softening and widening, as if massaged by the breath. Sense the twin gravita-

---

[*] www.jetli.com.
[†] Chögyam Trungpa, *Shambhala: The Sacred Path of the Warrior* (New York: Bantam Books, 1984).

tional pulls that tug the body groundward even as the upper areas simultaneously are lifted skyward. The principles in the Sitting Tune-Up are applicable to standing and walking as well.

Then, on an inhalation, raise one foot and let it extend forward half a foot length, beginning to exhale as it moves toward the ground and settles, like a tree being planted on the earth. Let your body weight remain on the foot on the ground. As your weight surrenders to the ground, take care that the body and head remain erect, rather than falling forward. As a subsequent inhale commences, lift your opposite foot and move forward, beginning to exhale as the foot comes to earth, as before, completing the exhalation as that foot is fully settled. It may help at first to use words like *lifting, moving,* and *placing* to accompany your foot movements. Let the weight of the torso and limbs drop continually, declaring a truce in the body's ongoing war with gravity.

When practicing the world body meditation, pause periodically, standing still to feel the interplay of gravity, body, and environment. Short pauses offer a taste of your body opening into the fullness of the world body. When Ezra and I offer retreats in natural settings that are conducive to outdoor meandering, walking periods are sometimes accompanied by silent words or a verse, a tradition we both came to appreciate when attending retreats with Thich Nhat Hanh, long before we met.

Here's a verse we used at a recent retreat in the Australian rain forest: "As I walk, the mind will wander; with each sound, the mind returns. As I breathe, the heart is open; with each step, I touch the earth." Ambling through the bush, with the untrained parrots in the trees providing backup music, we came across a fairly large python sunning on a log. Neither the people nor the python showed any visible agitation, as we snaked along, carried by the verse and the wonder of the vicinity—ticks, leeches, and all.

Why not experiment with your own words and saunter into kinship with the earth? At some point we may find kinesthetic confirmation of the words of Zen ancestor Shih-t'ou Hsi-ch'ien, from "The Identity of Relative and Absolute," an ideal verse to accompany walking: "If you do not see the Way, you do not see it even as you walk on it."

8 *Being-Awareness*

When we try to pick out anything by itself, we find it hitched to everything else in the universe. The sun shines not on us, but in us; the rivers flow not past, but through us.

JOHN MUIR

AFTER THE KOREAN WAR, my father took pictures all over the world, mailing back rolls of film as he traveled. All of them were blank, since a mechanical problem in his new camera closed the lens cover every time he took a picture. The human equivalent of this lens-cover malfunction is self-centered memory, the kind of planning and fantasizing that snaps awareness shut, as our ego thoughts block the view that life is offering at the moment. If it weren't for this phenomenon, we might not need meditation techniques to help us see through the mind's lens cover.

The exercises from the physical dimension help activate the experiencer, an embodied attunement to sensation, which interfaces with the open awareness dimension. Now we can make the acquaintance of the observer, which involves the ability to keep a spacious, objective eye on whatever appears—provided the view isn't obscured by self-centered thinking. Open awareness has a three-dimensional quality. Have you noticed that when you're not distracted, there's a different sound mix in each ear, just as there is with stereo speakers?

As the experiencer and observer coalesce into a team, they merge into *being awareness,* with an increased sense of undividedness. Our sense of identity grows more encompassing as a perceptual flip occurs, which allows the body and mind to be perceived as part of the scene, more of who we are than the ego's habitual role as star player on the stage.

People sometimes wonder why open awareness and the sense of being awareness don't develop naturally through immersion in nature, music, or art; shouldn't the grandeur pull us in, effortlessly? That can happen, but it usually doesn't last long; otherwise people who take the most vacations or attend art events regularly would be quite awake. Sadly, it sometimes seems as if all that pleasure drives people to meditation! What do you think brought me, a professional musician and music teacher, to zen? Ironically, the experiences we associate with good feelings sometimes keep us closer to obliteration than liberation. There's no problem with taking an occasional immersion bath in things we find enjoyable, as I sometimes do with music, as long as we don't equate this with being awake. Even if self-consciousness is absent for a while, the ego has hardly been transcended. It will soon be back, raring to go, like a child after a nap.

Zen has assured us for a millennium that as illusions fall away, there's a shift from self-as-person, to self-awareness, to self-as-awareness. Taking this as a working hypothesis, we still need to remember that it doesn't happen all at once; it's more likely to be a state that we visit, rather than our full-time home address, for quite a while.

BBSTSBB: A Palindrome

BBSTSBB is a palindrome composed of the first letters of seven words that beckon our awareness to open: balance, breathing, sensations, touch, senses, boundary, and boundlessness. We move from a sense of boundary, of being confined to what's inside our skin into the *boundlessness* of our surroundings and the open sky.

These seven checkpoints can provide some variety to our sense of awareness, tricking the easily bored mind into staying present a little longer than it might otherwise tolerate during meditation, and eventually the rest of life.

1. Balance. Feel your body surrounded by air. Notice your posture and balance.

2. Breathing. Feel the air in the body as you breathe, the movements of your torso filling and emptying.

3. Sensations. Scan your body for strong physical sensations, feeling them, as they are, for a few breaths.

4. Touch. Feel the subtle pressure or texture of the contact points between your feet and the floor, your hands and your lap.

5. Senses. Let your awareness open into the world of hearing, seeing, smelling, and tasting (even the inside of the mouth has a taste).

6. Boundary. Feel your total bodily gestalt or presence, including the body outline and everything within it.

7. Boundlessness. As these experiences infiltrate one another, let life's inclusivity have its way with you.

You can focus on the checkpoints individually, sequentially, or cumulatively. If considering seven checkpoints sounds daunting, choosing even one to pay attention to is practicing presence.

Experiencing, Inside Out: Coming to Our Senses

Years ago, I was driving American zen pioneer Flora Courtois across the New Mexico desert. After long hours of driving, a period of *just seeing* occurred—a seamless magnificence unbounded by the usual divisions and distortions. It was like *experiencing* turned inside out; in fact, the notions of outside and inside no longer pertained. However, quite soon the old familiar notions of space and time seeped back in, and I dared to venture, "Flora, did you know that you can see without thinking?" Flora's response: "Well, dear, how can you really *see* when you're thinking?" That pithy remark sent lifelong mental machinations into high gear, thoughts flying faster than the speed limit, as my ego tried to reclaim the driver's seat. Its siren screamed, "If you don't get back into your mind, you'll end up out of your mind!"

Experiencing as used here doesn't refer to "having experiences," instances where the veil of separation dissipates. In this case, experiencing means empirical, bodily-based sensuous awareness, a whiff of the unboundedness of life-without-borders. As our sensing function comes out of mothballs, life's shifting shapes, sounds, and stuff are experienced as energy and sensation—nothing cosmic, just ordinary. The body may feel porous, like a screen, through which things flow freely. However, there are those occasional wasps that stick in the screen. One such wasp, for some attendees at our recent Australian rain-forest retreat, was the sound of construction buzz saws that joined the natural calls of parrots and kook-aburras one morning. Mechanical sounds in the natural splendor can seem like actionable offenses, until we remember that our irritation is much harsher than the sounds themselves.

The likelihood of experiencing inside out increases as our senses are revitalized. Formerly mystifying phrases—like letting-be, non-doing, sur-render, and silence—start to literally "make sense." While the reality behind these phrases is always available, words can only point. The reality is ungraspable. It's not an it. It has no I. It can't be bottled or sold. You can't get a degree or credential in it. You can't even give it away free. Yet nothing could be more real.

Usually the process of coming to our senses, or experiencing without boundaries, isn't as dramatic as that desert example. Early tastes sometimes seem exceptionally powerful because they contrast so vividly with the dulling blinders that so often dim our vision. After all, the sensory world is always right here. We do, however, have a penchant for insular attention. It starts when we're toddlers, slithering toward anticipated delights and re-tracting, amoeba-like, from discomforts. Those early maneuverings are in-stinctual: if touch equals ouch, then avoid. As the brain develops, we add the oar of intellect, as we try to row our little boat to safe harbor in times of distress. The unbounded vitality that results from direct contact with life slowly deadens.

One of the casualties of unawareness in the sensory realm is common *sense,* which is a combination of mental acuity and practicality backed by sensorial perception. Without common sense, a lot of nonsense is guaranteed. In my twenties, I took a personality typology test and got a zero in the category called *sensation.* This meant that I hardly realized I was on the planet. The tester said, "If you don't work on that, you're going to get hit by a truck." I struggled to remedy this, borrowing a friend's dog for a few weeks, sniffing where it sniffed, cocking my head to hear sounds it detected. Four months later when I retook the test, my score had improved from zero to five, out of fifty possible points. The material world hadn't gone anywhere; I was just busily trying to think my way through life.

Here's a koan (in the sense of a question requiring an experiential rather than an intellectual response) that can help probe awareness into the open: "If thoughts of separation don't arise, where could separation possibly exist?" The fact that things look different doesn't mean they're separate. The dawning of open awareness ushers in a vitality we haven't known since childhood.

We can also question the limitations we have applied to words and ideas like *silence;* rather than being limited to an absence of sounds or thinking, consider the quiet when the ego's incessant voice-over is silent, and the mind's strident sound track doesn't block the actual sounds of life. As the sounds of silence whisper and shout, the senses expand, ever more able to perceive that the tiniest tingle is a diving board into our whole nature.

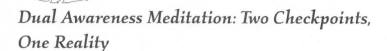

Dual Awareness Meditation: Two Checkpoints, One Reality

> The Dharma-realm of true actuality harbors neither self nor other.
> To reach accord with it at once, just say, "Not two!"
> SENG-TS'AN

Of all the techniques in our awareness toolbox, the Dual Awareness meditation is one of the best for experiencing simultaneous awareness of the body and the environment. By uniting the observer and the experiencer, which we've already met, we have a practical bridge from our meditation seat to the street and, as the dual checkpoints entice awareness into merging into one reality, to the third Zen ancestor's "not two."

Dual Awareness: The Meditation

Let your body settle, fluctuating slightly to remain supple. As your weight sinks earthward, feel the head and upper torso floating. For several rounds of breathing, feel the flexibility of the spine elongating and softening.

During this meditation, in the beginning, *strongly decline thoughts*. Rarely do we suggest this; however, for awareness to take hold in the sensory and the physical realms, thoughts will be asked to step aside for at least the first part of the meditation.

Tune in on the following, for several breaths each:

- The breathing in the head area—the coolness of the air entering your nose, and the subtle texture of the exhale
- The breathing in the chest—the rising and falling, and the slight movements of your shoulders and back
- The breathing in the abdomen—the expanding and contracting currents of your breath
- The overall experience of breathing—the sensations of air in the head and nose area, the chest, and the abdomen, all together, for a few more breaths

Now, bring the awareness to your breathing in the middle of the torso, and after a few breaths:

- Expand your attention to include the environmental ambience.
- Let awareness alternate between the breathing sensations and the environment.
- If possible, try to experience the combination of breathing-environment-air-sounds as an entirety.
- Let all of the above become a backdrop, about a quarter of your attention, with central breathing being the main anchor for attention.
- When sounds call out for attention, listen with the whole body, not just the ears, feeling the reverberations as they shimmer through your body.
- Listen to the almost silent sound of the breath, and the sounds between the sounds.

- When thoughts or emotions come along, for now simply notice them and return to dual awareness (later there will be further instructions on this).
- When awareness departs, invite it back with the *three-breath return policy,* one breath each for: feeling the breathing sensation, sensing the environment, and experiencing both simultaneously. Then, resume alternating between the various checkpoints.
- Let your consciousness be immersed in the all-encompassing mix of sensations, senses, and spaciousness for as long as you like.

In addition to the checkpoints used above, you can use other awareness points. Be sure to maintain dual awareness, including one bodily sensation and one observation from the menu of sensory phenomena to ensure that inside out awareness is activated. One effective mix is wedding your strongest bodily sensation to awareness of the air temperature.

Unlocking the Paradox

Dual awareness helps undercut some of the perniciously painful dichotomies we've fallen into: when entering a room full of people, the radar goes on: is it safe or unsafe? A sensation is felt—is it desirable or undesirable? A sound—is it pleasant or unpleasant? We can even chop our so-called self in two: "I'm special; I'm worthless," or both, if we're precocious. Dual awareness offers plenty of breathing room for discomforts that we might otherwise be unwilling to tolerate during meditation and beyond.

As dual awareness pervades our life increasingly, it can accommodate whatever the day presents: freeway driving, bad hair days, and time spent outdoors—the transitions are smoothed as open awareness becomes their common meeting ground. There's plenty of room for occasional solos from the mind's top hits, which, after all, are part of the interweaving harmony of life. But they no longer have to drown out the rest of the band.

As dual awareness illuminates the sea of undifferentiated sensation, we open into a leap at the heart of zen practice, into the unknowing that has been spoken of in spiritual texts for millenia. When we're new to the territory, it can seem more of a tumble than a leap. Yet having the seemingly solid ground slip away from beneath our feet is the best way to embrace the sky.

9 *Untrain Your Parrot*

**The unleashed power of the atom has changed everything save our
modes of thinking and we thus drift toward unparalleled catastrophe
... If only I had known, I would have become a watchmaker.**
ALBERT EINSTEIN

A COUPLE WAS ENJOYING an intimate moment. Person A
whispered some sweet nothings in Person B's ear, whereupon Person B said, "Be quiet!" Person A, hurt, stopped whispering and asked later,
"Why did you say to be quiet?" Person B responded, "You were interfering
with my fantasy."

This is what can happen when thinking runs nonstop. When our mind
heads for the past, future, or fantasy—as in this example—rampant thinking diminishes enjoyment of our favorite things, such as nature walks,
vacations, sexual activity, or visits with friends.

Thinking occupies strange turf in the spiritual world. Belief-oriented groups have faith in things that can't be confirmed empirically, and some thoughts are accorded high status. The meditative traditions often wash up on the other end of the beach, sometimes going so far as to look down on thinking. Twelfth-century Japan's Zen ancestor Dogen Zenji stirred up a hornet's nest by saying "Think non-thinking." Fold in Zen's notorious mind-stopping koans and Bodhidharma's injunction not to rely on words and scriptures, and thinking and talking end up low on the pyramid.

At least as early as Epictetus, a Greek philosopher, it has been pointed out that we're not so much disturbed by things as the views we hold of them. The gossamer web of thinking may be as delicate and insubstantial as a spiderweb, yet it can just as easily snag all sorts of things in its clutches. The magnetic field of awareness has a way of pulling into consciousness all sorts of thought-filings, things we filed and forgot, some quite shocking. Properly understood, the mind can help clarify itself, through objective observation of our most suspicious thoughts and belief systems.

Mental weather may be as insubstantial as a cloudbank, yet it is just as capable of obscuring the view. As we inspect our contradictory and ephemeral thoughts, we start to fathom their full-empty nature, even if only intellectually at first. Continued observation brings a dawning realization: the chaos and limitations of a thought-based ego structure can't begin to do justice to the profundity of our actual nature, heartmind.

Sorting Out Thinking Modes: Objective and Subjective Categories

To shed some discernment on thinking, and the speech that arises from it, we can sort thinking's panoply of modes into the broad categories of objective and subjective thinking. You could say that all thinking is subjective, since it is funneled through a conditioned human brain; however, our objective category will include technical thinking, culturally agreed-upon data, names of objects, symbolic systems like math and science, and the sixth sense we have already met—impersonal thinking that describes and relates to experiential situations.

The subjective category will include opinions, beliefs, speculation, hypotheses, and the ability to reflect on and express things that move us. Much of our thinking has been influenced by our trained parrot's presuppositions, so we're probably prone to confuse description and facts with diagnosis and interpretation. Here's an intriguing irony for you: even though one of our chief preoccupations is entertaining thoughts, we're remarkably reluctant to entertain the thought that spiritual training requires the objective scrutiny of thinking. Could this skittishness be symptomatic of the ego's desire to avoid detection? Zen folks are well acquainted with the rapidity with which cogitation usurps meditation; we decide to meditate, and our mind gallops off into unbridled thinking. Then, the very mind that took a field trip turns tail and snaps, "Stop thinking, you're supposed to be meditating!"

Subjective thinking can't be our tool of choice in wending our way through this morass, since that would be tantamount to giving elementary students free rein over a classroom. Objective thinking is a better choice, because it's a close relative of the observer and open awareness.

Learning to eavesdrop on our foggy and inaccurate thinking through meditation can stave off a lot of misery, as we discover that thoughts are no more than thoughts. We don't have to go to war with thoughts or attempt to have better ones. More effective is attentive, respectful awareness. As we learn to listen, we're more likely to engage in mindful consideration before rushing headlong into the actions or opinions our thoughts espouse.

Tangled Thinking: A Worksheet

Tangled thinking gives thinking a bad name. A plant called kudzu clogs the waterways of Mississippi's Yazoo River so completely that the Yazoo is almost impassable to boats. The phrase "kudzu on the Yazoo" has become idiomatic for anything that is so tangled that almost nothing can get through. Another factor in tangled thinking is the cognitive *splat* that sometimes occurs after an emotional shock. Our mind shuts down, similar to the way physical shock shuts down bodily processes, and we lose contact with the genuine intelligence that is ordinarily available. We're left blank and bewildered. These factors constitute a large part of our parrot's training, and as the tangles take up residence in our mental repertoire, they form a filter that usurps our capacity to perceive things directly.

See which of these thinking tangles are among your favorites. Some of the following categories overlap, as you might expect with tangles:

Past think (memory). Mulling over remembered events, including those that never happened, at least not the way we recall.

Future think (planning). Trying to get a jump on the next moment. Some planning is practical, but not the kind that resembles boarding a plane that hasn't yet reached the runway.

Novocain mind. Using thinking to drown out unpleasant sensations or emotions, or even undesirable thoughts—such as thinking about a career change to drown out thoughts of being a failure.

False cause. Assuming that we know exactly what caused something. This ignores the intermingling factors and is a major control strategy, which is hard to see until it breaks down.

Sick body = sick mind. An example of *false cause* thinking that is so popular that it deserves a separate heading. The belief is that if we're physically sick, it means there's something that we're not looking at, or that our mind or emotions are out of whack. We now have two sicknesses: sick body *and* sick mind!

Fantasy. Spending time in daydreams, imagination, and fabrication.

Chat room. Focusing on personal conversations, online and between our ears.

Opinions masquerading as data. Assuming that our strong opinions are facts. This is easy to spot when someone else does it, especially if we disagree: think sports, politics, religion.

My truth. Believing a subset of the above: "My truth is that you're insensitive."

Feely think (feelings as facts). Confusing emotions and thinking: when someone says "I feel that you . . . ," you know that an opinion is coming, not a feeling or data. It's easy to make our subjective thoughts justify our worldview of lifestyle: "I know it's true; I just feel it."

Complaint addict. Finding fault, focusing on what's wrong.

Put-downs. Making comments that devalue a person or situation, intentionally or unintentionally.

"And that's bad." Leaving an often-unspoken negative PS tailing after an opinion.

Rushing to judgment. Making decisions based on little or no evidence.

Prejudice. Prejudging, literally. Justifying the denigration of individuals or groups, or attributing negative traits to them, sometimes without ever having met one.

No middle ground. Holding extreme views like "If you're not for us, you're against us." The ego's version is a flip-flop between feeling superior (or special) and worthless: "I'm nothing; I'm special."

Double standard. Holding others accountable in areas where we excuse ourselves: "I'm laid back; you're lazy. I'm assertive; you're bossy." "People shouldn't do the crazy things they do. Oh, I do some crazy things but I can't help it; it's because of my childhood."

Assumptions and expectations. Having hidden agendas and unspoken "shoulds" that we only notice when they're not met. Common versions in spiritual circles include the following:

> *True believer.* Thinking we need an authority figure or group to tell us what to believe (or do).

> *Magical thinking.* Believing that certain thoughts, words, or actions will produce a desired outcome. "If I meditate faithfully, good things will happen to me." When others indulge in magical thinking, we call it superstition; when it's ours, we call it belief or truth.

> *False hope—false hopelessness.* Expecting spiritual practice, relationships, or jobs to provide something that they can't offer, such as an answer to a problem or endless equanimity. Such hopes are almost always replaced at some point by false hopelessness, like "Practice doesn't work."

> *Mind reading, insistence on treating intuition as factual.*

Assuming we know what others think or feel about things that aren't substantiated by physical evidence or verbal confirmation; if we involve intuition, we must do so with care.

Babbling brook. Occupying the mind with a barrage of seemingly innocuous thoughts.

Formulaic responses. Talking the zen talk: "Well, of course I label thoughts. Then I experience bodily sensations. Then I hear environmental sounds. I'm right here now." Really? Maybe we've retrained our parrot to say the zen thing?

Culturally approved tangled thinking. Feeling entitled and justified to react in a particular way to a situation. For example, "I can't be happy unless, or until, I have a particular job, relationship, living situation, or acceptable children or parents" or "My life should be free from pain."

Total thinking write-off. Deciding that thinking is deluded and attempting to let go of thoughts. This only works through repression or anesthesia, or thoughts would have stopped running long ago!

Concentration

Concentration allows the mind to settle so that attention can focus on one point. Without concentration, it would be almost impossible to learn skills, retain information, or perform activities. We wouldn't want a brain surgeon operating on our brain while planning a golf game; we'd want him or her concentrating—on our brain only.

The ability to concentrate is innate, and as with most abilities, some people are more inclined toward concentration than are others. Because we tend to get lost in every passing thought, this is likely to impinge on our ability to concentrate. Our early attempts at concentration make it obvious how determined the mind is to engage in unbridled thinking. One of our first steps will be to acknowledge the obvious: that concentration is frequently absent. Even longtime meditators report coming to with a jolt when a bell signals the end of a meditation period, when they had thought they were in deep concentration but may have been lost in daydreams or a trancelike state.

How can this be? Didn't we learn to concentrate when we crammed for tests in school? Considering how little we retained, even from classes we aced, it's possible that rather than developing concentration as a seed of awakening, we were relying on our ability to function under pressure, heavily dosed with caffeine, procrastination, and desperation.

Concentration has many legitimate applications, including carrot chopping, which is a popular topic of zen stories and is well known to kitchen workers at retreats. Concentration develops best when we use checkpoints to which our attention can return when it departs. There are many options, including mantras, visualizations, chanting, and altering the breath, all of which involve adding a number, picture, or word to what's going on at the time. It helps if the concentration object is somewhat uninteresting, since otherwise we may be engaging in fascination rather than actualizing concentration.

Misuses of concentration abound, since by definition it tunes out quite a bit. In my early meditation days, I enlisted concentration to avoid leg pain, continuing my childhood habit of avoiding discomfort by placing attention elsewhere. It succeeded in tuning out the pain to some extent. However, there are repercussions: first, you can hurt yourself. Second, forcefully turning attention away from discomfort strengthens the notion that escapism is a viable option. Our scheme will fall flat when something inescapable shows up, like an intractable illness, loss of a loved one, or a major life upheaval. When we're in a weakened or vulnerable condition, concentration is often difficult or impossible. If we use concentration to try to block thinking, the thoughts may indeed step aside for a while. But the thoughts, rather than going away, have headed for the basement (suppression) or the attic (our habitual head trips). When we stop forcing them into obeisance, they will rebound, usurping awareness, invigorated by their time offline.

Another dubious temptation that I continued to appease regularly as a novice meditator was to use concentration to induce altered states or absorption. Seeking rapid enlightenment, concentration was my tool of choice after reading Wu-Men's commentary on the koan "Wu," or emptiness ("Mu" in Japanese). It says: "Don't you want to pass through the barrier? Then concentrate yourself into this Mu, with your 84,000 pores, making your whole body one great inquiry."* I had some intense moments, but they faded fast, and all hell broke loose in their wake.

Concentration is not a complete practice in itself, in that it doesn't allow us to open to life as a whole, as attested to by Jon Kabat-Zinn: "Concentration practice, however strong and satisfying, is incomplete without mindfulness to complement and deepen it. By itself it resembles a state of withdrawal from the world."†

Nonetheless, concentration is invaluable as a component of a comprehensive practice, starting with its ability to help us stay put, even in adverse circumstances. Concentration, in combination with methods

* Zenkei Shibayama, *Zen Comments on the Mumonkan* (New York: Harper Collins, 1984).
† Jon Kabat-Zinn, *Wherever You Go, There You Are* (New York: Hyperion Press, 1994).

for developing mindfulness and awareness, can allow more of life to get in.

Breath Counting: A Meditation

Breath counting is one of the best-known tools for developing meditative concentration. The commonest form is to number your breathing, usually from one to ten. Say the number silently on an exhale, then simply inhale. If you space out completely or get to 150, go back to one. Most people report that they rarely get beyond three before they get lost in thoughts, so take heart. Most of your attention stays on the numbers, with enough awareness of your breathing sensations to know when to change numbers. Counting provides instant feedback when your attention strays, an on-ramp to return to the concentration highway.

A more physiologically grounded form of breath counting focuses primarily on the physical feeling of breathing. The numbers provide a backdrop to help attention stay on target. Keeping the focus on sensations like this counteracts the tendency to "breathe by the numbers" and miss the sensuous nature of breathing.

Breath counting's greatest advantage is that it is undramatic and always available. If your counting becomes mechanical or you can mentally write your novel while counting and not lose a beat, try counting backward. You can't fail breath counting, since even the awareness of being unable to get beyond three *is* awareness. There are no contests in breath counting, so rather than stewing over which form of breath counting is best, just inhale, and on the next exhale say "one."

10 Fingers Pointing at the Moon

MINDFUL ACTIVITY LABELING

> The present situation has to be faced completely, opened to with mindfulness . . . you must be willing to let life itself become your teacher.
>
> JON KABAT-ZINN

AN APHORISM THAT IS well known in zen in the wake of a haiku by Basho reminds us not to mistake the finger pointing at the moon for the moon itself.* This is a layered teaching, reminding us to distinguish the map from the territory, and to remember the point,

* R. H. Blyth, *Basho Haiku* (Tokyo: Hokseido Press, 1949).

encountering our profound nature—which is the heart of the territory. With spiritual practice it's often easy to take refuge in descriptive words, not realizing that we haven't reached the actual domain pointed to by the words.

Zen is replete with fingers pointing to the big picture, or the full-empty dimension, particularly koans that thwart the linear mind, like "Show me your face before your parents' birth." Such pointers can take us the necessary distance; however, along the way, we also need fingers that point to the profundity of mundane daily activities, in comprehensible fashion, since we're unlikely to recognize their numinous full-empty dimension unless we're substantially grounded on the earth beneath our feet.

One of the most practical fingers to help us along is *mindful activity labeling,* which uses words to align our mind with the activity at hand. The most succinct labeling uses action words, especially words ending in "ing," like lifting, moving, and chewing. These words point toward nonduality by summing up an event in a single word. Consider the difference between saying "I am driving my car" and simply saying "Driving," which takes the "I" out of the driver's seat. Driving can unfold with simple awareness, without putting the emphasis on the "I." After all, isn't it this "I" that loses sight of road conditions and sometimes chooses revenge over skillful driving? "He cut me off; I'll show him."

Mindful activity labeling isn't a haiku-esque replacement for ordinary conversation. It's a silent, temporary practice prop, an escort returning our mind to the action of the moment.

Meditation retreats are often laced with mindful activity labeling during walking and eating periods, to counterbalance the mind's tendency to spin off into a smorgasbord of enticements. During a meal, we engage mindful activity labeling by silently saying the "ing" words that relate to eating: lifting, chewing, tasting, swallowing, thinking, cutting, dropping. As each word is said, we feel the physical movement and the sensation it reflects. If this process sounds artificial, compare it with what the mind usually does during meals. If saying the word "chewing" silently and eating at the same time seems too bothersome, maybe our brain is out to lunch?

Mindful activity labeling functions somewhat like a Greek chorus: when the characters onstage are walking across a bridge, the chorus marches out and says, "They are now walking across a bridge." Even if it seems redundant, the process counteracts the ego's disdain for attending to simple activities. People can be disconcerted to discover that after making great efforts to attend retreats, they can spend an entire morning meditation session thinking about lunch. Then during lunch, attention heads toward the upcoming afternoon break. When the break arrives, we use it to strategize about how to get through the afternoon. (Someone I know recently signed up to attend a retreat after forgetting a commitment to lead a mindfulness workshop elsewhere that same weekend!)

Mindful activity labeling provides ballast to anchor our attention where we are. Over time it helps us digest the fact that eating isn't divided into *me* on the narrow end of the fork and *not-me,* the bite on the other end. Then, as awareness is resuscitated, the -ing words can fall away naturally, much as a cocoon drops off when it's no longer needed, allowing the butterfly of life-as-it-is to float free.

Thought Echoing: Directly Untraining Our Parrot

If we're not trying to retrain our parrot, our conditioned mind, what helps the untraining, or unconditioning, process occur most naturally? Poetry and folk wisdom stress the value of seeing ourselves as others see us. Now that open awareness has helped activate the observer, and some exposure to the physical dimension has enlivened the experiencer, the condition makes more embodied objective awareness available. Now it's time to listen carefully to what our parrot is already saying. This may sound unnecessary, since we're thinking and talking all the time, but how often are we really listening?

One way to begin to attend more carefully to what the mind is up to, before it moves into speech, is *thought echoing,* which helps us discover the content of our minds by actively mirroring back thoughts precisely. This is done primarily during formal meditation.

Thought echoing starts as soon as we notice that thinking has taken over. We listen to what we are thinking and echo it back verbatim, the way a trained parrot repeats a phrase in rote fashion, preceded by the word "thinking": if the thought is "Won't thought echoing make me think more?" the echo would be "*Thinking* 'Won't thought echoing make me think more?'"

When I first started using thought echoing, I was sure that the speed of my thinking had doubled. Actually, the echoing was only mirroring back the deluge of thoughts that used to pass unnoticed. Far from increasing the volume of thoughts, echoing slows the rate by setting up a temporary roadblock in the oncoming thought traffic.

Thought echoing has the added value of providing snapshots of the mind's specific content. This in turn discloses, over time, whether our thinking is primarily functional and life-serving, or self-serving, by providing a specific script of our ego structure. Ego is always specific; someone once asked pioneering nutritionist Adele Davis whether apricots were good for you, and she said, "Which apricot, where?" Which ego, where? The thoughts will tell.

Thought echoing not only keeps the notion of an ego from becoming vaguely generic, it also pinpoints the mind's inconsistencies. It's common to hold, and believe equally, two opposing thoughts: "I must do whatever is suggested to me," and "I absolutely must not do anything that is suggested to me." Stereo dissonance like this ties us in mental and physical knots. We may be discomfited to find some *bottom feeders*—truly unpleasant thoughts about ourselves and others, thoughts whose presence we might have been able to deny before thought echoing brought them to light. After thought echoing has become a stable ability, we can start to employ thought *labeling,* by category: conversing, daydreaming, reminiscing, planning, and rehashing. Unlike thought echoing, thought labeling requires additional thinking, so we should wait until we've become familiar with our general thought patterns before trying thought labeling. After the content and patterns of our thinking are quite well known to us, it's sometimes enough to say "thinking" silently, as a form of thought awareness. Still, both thought echoing and thought labeling may need to be in our repertoire for quite a while.

As thoughts become more transparent, it's fun to play with other forms of thought awareness. For example, when upsets come along, we can ask, "What's my most believed thought about this?" A follow-up question might be "What would I like to have said?" Or, "What disturbs me most about this situation?" Then pause and listen for about a second. Another question is, "What am I most afraid will happen?"

One of my most enjoyable ways of hearing thoughts came to me one semester when I was teaching a music class. One day when I entered the classroom, the students had already been having a group gripe about a math class. I said that if they wanted to complain, they could sing their complaints. That slowed the grumbling, and those who persisted were asked to sing. I even joined in on the piano and we had a blues jam. A few students confessed that they hadn't realized how much they complained until they were faced with the singing assignment.

For a while I assigned jukebox numbers to my most predictable thoughts: A2 on the jukebox was "No Matter How Hard I Try, They'll Always Think I'm Inadequate." After hundreds of labelings, this technique has effectively taken most of the juice out of my parrot's top ten tunes. Using thought echoing and labeling with garden-variety thoughts helps us recognize the tough customers, the ones that are central to our identity and worldview. It will become obvious that the problem isn't the thoughts; it's not recognizing that they have taken charge.

Now that we have met the mental dimension's echoer, it can collaborate with open awareness's observer and the physicality of the experiencer. There's an old proverb about a mother watching a child play with its toys: the mother represents the combined wisdom of the observer, experiencer, and echoer; the child represents the ego self, which can no longer run things with so much abandon; and the toys are the strategies and imaginings that keep our trained parrot from discovering its actual nature.

Thought Trees: An Exercise

Visual tools have been used to classify and clarify since the neo-Platonist Porphyry diagrammed Aristotle's Categories. In what is now called "Porphyry's Tree," he united the logical, linguistic, and spatial modes of functioning.*

Thought Trees take Porphyry's version as their ancestor. Writing things down in a visually oriented format provides more tangibility than leaving the ideas to float like leaves in the mind stream and allows the mental dimension to be enhanced by physical and open awareness.

You need a sheet of 8 x 11 inch (or larger) paper, a pencil, and possibly colored markers if you want to get artistic. When an event precipitates a mental avalanche, write the main theme at the bottom of a piece of paper, to be the root of the tree. Then, without pausing to ponder, write your random thoughts all over the page. Include any sensations or emotions that come up as you reflect on the root.

For example, you hear that someone is ridiculing you behind your back. The root could be "being ridiculed." Supporting thoughts, which you write down lickety-split, might include "friends turn on me," "not appreciated," or "hopeless." If you notice a tight jaw, queasy stomach, or shame, jot them down as well.

Later, as you look over the tree, you may notice things on the page that are major factors—the trunk and branches. Other things that are lighter weight are the foliage. To reveal the structure underlying the

---

* Jonathan Barnes, ed. *Cambridge Companion to Aristotle* (Cambridge, U.K.: Cambridge University Press, 1995).

seemingly miscellaneous entries, you can use different colored pens for things that seem to be trunk, branches, and leaves. As you start to draw lines and circles, don't worry if your tree starts to resemble Porphyry's bush! Connecting lines may start to reveal how elements intermesh in your issue. The sheer acts of drawing and writing add consciousness to the mix, without any need to analyze the whys and wherefores.

The items that seem significant are likely to include the heavy hitters in our conditioning, even the Loch Ness monsters that emerge and submerge regularly, making them hard to spot as they wend their way through our unconscious. These thoughts require extensive echoing.

Items can be added later. Occasionally an "Aha!" may shoot forth, as we spot evidence of our trained parrot. Thought Trees focus on the mental and physical dimensions, against the backdrop of open awareness. The emotional dimension makes its contributions as well, and the full-empty dimension starts to sneak in as we see the insubstantiality or even opposing content of some of the entries.

Journaling for Awareness: A Worksheet

Journaling, like Thought Trees, keeps the mental dimension from existing solely between our ears. Many people keep a journal or diary, which is an excellent source of information about the mind's processes, with dialog from the trained parrot interspersed among the profundities.

Journaling for Awareness—writing down the gristle—lets us literally highlight some of our entrenched, indigestible thoughts. We start in a quiet place, with a journal and pen in hand, and follow these instructions.

1. *Contemplate the gristle.* Raise the question, "What seems to be most dissatisfying right now?" That's the gristle.

2. *List items.* To the gristle-laden issues you write in your journal, add others from your mind. Reiterate the question periodically: "What seems to be most dissatisfying?" The order of the items doesn't matter; keep writing nonstop for about five minutes.

3. *Pick one item.* Choose one item on your list that jumps out.

4. *Observe.* Setting pen and paper aside, adopt a stable posture. Tune in on the environment, the objects in your vicinity, and your bodily sensations.

5. *Taste the gristle.* Consider the item you have chosen as if you were a scientist looking at a specimen under a microscope. Can you be objective about it, as if it pertained to someone else? Consider the item again briefly, and then move on.

6. *Reflect on bodily gristle.* Do any distasteful bodily feelings come up as you reflect on the item? Feel whatever is present now.

7. *Reflect on mental and emotional gristle.* As you continue to feel your bodily sensations, do any unpalatable emotions or thoughts arise? Within a few seconds, move on.

8. *Put the gristle on hold.* The mental gristle related to this item is no longer the focal point of your attention, yet it's not suppressed.

9. *Let the bodily gristle digest.* Return to the palpable physical

quality of the present, your bodily sense of presence, the writing surface, and the gristle.

10. Let it all be. You can remain in inclusive awareness or return to what the day needs.

11 *The Many Me's of Identity*

FROM EGO TO INSTRUMENT OF AWAKENING

To study the Way of Awakening is to study the self. To study the self is
to see through the self. To see through the self is to be awakened as all
existence.

ZEN ANCESTOR DOGEN ZENJI

IDENTITY IS CENTRAL TO spiritual discussions, since it is the
crucible from which many of our mental concepts evolve—notions
like divinity, salvation, reward and punishment, life and death, and the
basic nature of existence. One of the central tasks of zen training is to learn
the difference between concepts that have to be taken on faith and postu-
lations to be tested in the white-hot forge of practice and life.

Ideas like this one, from the Apostle's Creed, demand belief: "Jesus rose from the dead and sits at the right hand of the Father,"* while this one invites firsthand testing: "What you do for the least of them [the poor and outcasts] you do for me,"† attributed to Jesus in the New Testament. These words are the equivalent of a zen koan, requiring us to reflect on an identity sufficiently vast to include the unity of Jesus, the poorest—and ourselves.

Lines like the following two phrases may sound sectarian because of their terminology, but could it be that they point us to the very place where we stand, asking us to recognize our true self: "The kingdom of God is within; the kingdom of heaven at hand"‡ and "This very place is the Lotus Land, his very body, the Buddha."§

We interpret such statements based on our sense of identity. Until we learn to contemplate such ideas, to see whether they can be savored and digested, we're likely to construe them in ways that keep us encased within a narrow identity. Let's face it; a large part of what we regard as our actual self consists of mental constructs, so we will consider identity as a subset of the mental dimension.

The implications of the ego (the self, or "I am" in Latin) differ somewhat in spirituality and psychology, both tinged with some degree of narcissistic attachment to a truncated self. This Gospel of Myself that we keep resuscitating usually reduces down to being little more than a piece of protoplasm with a history.

* Episcopal Book of Common Prayer (New York: Church Hymnal Corporation, 1979).
† Matthew 25.
‡ Luke 17; Matthew 4.
§ Hakuin Ekaku Zenji, Zen Center San Diego Service Book.

Nondual auspices like zen may ⌐_____   ⌐ere is no separate
self, and nothing but the self, fror   ⌐rspective; however,
that paradigm has plenty of roor   ⌐ self, one that we can
call "me" for convenience. We nec⌐   ⌐mind, though, that our
"me" is composed of the same intangible ⌐ ⌐egates as everything else,
fulfilling its practical roles, as a sensing, thinking, and exploring instrument par excellence. The process of awakening may well confirm that ⌐ our self is awareness itself and is in no way cut off from the earth, sky, and sea.

What does it take for us to see that we're not merely case histories with predictable patterns? When Dogen Zenji reminds that we need to study the self in order to see through its limitations, he's exhorting us to awaken *as* all existence—to experience the unboundedness of our identity. Seeing our many me's is bound to bring a deeper appreciation of how Walt Whitman owned up to our plethora of me's in "Song of Myself": "Do I contradict myself? Very well then . . . I am large—I contain multitudes."* We recognize how varied the identities are that we adopt with coworkers, family members, freeway drivers, confidantes, and those who done us dirt. We wall off some identities from each other, and they hardly suspect one another's presence.

It's painful to be captured in the Venus flytrap of our ego; we know, on some level, how dissatisfying it is to keep trying to unearth a miniscule self from our archaeological dig of memories and strategic gambits. Along the way, we'll need to stay particularly alert to two enticing trails that border the path and prove to be dead ends: on one side, there's an aversion to ego

* Walt Whitman, *Song of Myself*, ed. Stephen Mitchell (Boston: Shambhala Publications, 1993).

investigation, which is sometimes denigrated in spiritual venues as an indulgence in delusion or psychologizing. On the other side is the reverse, an effort to turn ego stuff into the main dish on the spiritual menu. When we do this, it diminishes the path of awakening to little more than meditative therapy.

As our limited-edition identities are unmasked, whatever is genuine will withstand scrutiny. Walt Whitman's poem includes an expansively succinct claim: "I am deathless," pointing us toward the portals through which genuine love and gratitude can pass freely.

Many Me's: An Inventory of Essence and Ego Identity Traits

The groupings below reflect many qualities with which we might identify at a particular time. One way to start to open up the narrow confines of our cubicle is to regard this inventory as a rainbow, one in which we partake of all the colors. No longer do we need to claim to be only red, while referring to someone else as no more than blue.

Not all of the qualities in any group will fit, since so many factors operate together to produce our "individuality." Our responses will provide information for the exercises in this section. Circle the categories whose qualities seem to describe you best.

- Perfectionistic, imperfectionistic (looking for what's wrong), live in accord with my values, orderly, maintain strong internal standards for self and others

- Nurturing, helpful, occasional martyr, caring, "give to get," help-aholic, placing others' needs above my own and ignore mine in the process
- Seek esteem through achievements, overachiever or workaholic, motivational (of myself and others), preoccupied with my latest project
- Sensitive, aesthetic, misunderstood, nature loving, easily hurt, empathic, motivated by feelings and moods, unique, sometimes attracted to suffering
- Observant, analytical, conceptual orientation, interested in synthesizing broad perspectives, figure things out (including feelings), eccentric, sometimes stingy with my resources and feelings
- Loyal, dutiful, confused, indecisive, responsible, ambivalent toward authority figures (alternating between deferential and counterphobic), strongly motivated by security, often worried or anxious, fearful of apparent danger or tempted to flip into fascination with it
- Multifaceted enthusiasms; fun, fun, fun to be with; more interested in seeking than in finding; bon vivant; readily dissatisfied with work, relationships, and locale; quick to plummet from emotional highs
- Assertive boss or leader, champion of the underdog, justice seeker, player at the top and in power-based positions, my way or the highway
- Peacemaker; concerned with harmony; laid back; occasionally negligent; don't worry, be happy stance; chameleon-like; sometimes stubborn if demands are either made or perceived; may say yes and mean no; passive or passive-aggressive; daydreamer
- Other

Nature, Nurture, Neurosis, True Nature: Exploring the Anatomy of a Self

The self itself is the world; the self itself is the "I"; the self itself is God; all is the Supreme Self.

RAMANA MAHARSHI

As we move from infancy to autobiography, we adopt many notions of who we are, most of which boil down to a conglomerate of memories, reflections in a mirror, mind states, bodily functions, and behaviors. If there's no sense of an infinite identity, which zen describes with phrases like *a vast ocean of dazzling light,* it may seem catastrophic when the high waves of current events threaten to capsize our tiny ship of self. We try to keep the accumulated flotsam of our identity afloat, using it as water wings, not realizing we're already in the midst of the all-inclusive ocean of our actual being.

Let's have some fun, hypothesizing how this state of affairs might have come about. One thing is indubitable: observing newborns confirms that they don't arrive as tabulae rasae, little computers awaiting programming. Some burble and babble from day one, and others seem to arrive irritable or spaced out: "Even as a baby, he was mellow," "She was sociable from the beginning," "He's always had that solitary streak." If three children are present when Mommie throws dinner at the wall, one will cry, one will placate, and one will disappear. We seem to come down the chute equipped with particular traits that we will call *nature.*

It's said that babies seem to regard everything as an extension of themselves—almost the opposite of zen's "nothing but the self"—as if one's identity were extended or projected onto everything else, rather than seeing the self *as* everything.

Before age two, after we've bumped our heads a few times, or screamed, and no one appears, children start to draw a line between themselves and the world, designating the part that got hurt (or didn't get its way) as the self, and anything that looks threatening or nonaffirming becomes not-self, namely, almost everything.

Interactions with caretakers form a conglomerate of genetics and nature, which we will call *nurture:* child rearing, health conditions, diet, environment, socioeconomic factors, gender, and cultural conditioning for starters. As nature and nurture intermingle, the baby develops a repertoire of attitudes and behaviors that eventually coalesce into a virtual Halloween mask, whose purpose is to answer the question, "Who and how do I have to be?" Ergo, ego.

As the undeveloped brain mulls things over, some of the *nature and nurture* factors morph into an increasingly artificial blend, which we will call *neurosis,* just to keep the *n*'s coming. The reflective, solitary baby has episodes of withdrawal; the laid-back infant drifts off into the ozone; sociable little ones become manipulative; emotionally oriented tots occasionally resemble drama kings or queens; and reflective old souls can look world-weary. All before age three.

By kindergarten, most of us are unfailingly predictable. A glance through the family album highlights the shift, when the joy of smiling at an adult turns into approval seeking. Or the determination to tie our shoes all by ourselves becomes grim insistence on doing everything perfectly.

If our basic style is compliant rather than withdrawn or aggressive, we're more likely to acquire the template set forth by our early family and our societal, religious, and educational influences. Whatever attire we assume, our self-identity will bear stylistic similarities to our essence or nature traits, even after we start to color outside the lines. Our qualities and facades are likely to be so consistent that various psychospiritual systems and typologies have been able to describe them categorically over the centuries: Tibetan Buddhism's wisdom energies, the Enneagram, Jungian archetypes, the Zodiac, and others. Despite their limitations, when used with discernment, some of these resources can be informative in magnifying our objective awareness of the consistency of the ego's dimensions. An example of the potential usefulness of tools for dismantling our attachment to the qualities we identify with is that, even after years of therapy, becoming a recovering therapist, being involved in bodywork, zen, and myriad other modalities, I was sobered to see a list of qualities I thought were unique to me published in a book. Was "I" so transparent?

It's easy to forget the point of such enquiry, which is to see through our ego edifice. The nagging feeling that there's something missing in us leads to the almost irresistible enticement to rehash our childhood or attempt to attribute our present circumstances to historical happenings: "People tell me I'm hypersensitive. You would be too, if you'd been in my family." Statements like that can't possibly be true, or everyone with a distant dad would have the same perspective on life. Nor does everyone who goes through a tragic event come out with the same attitudes about it.

Looking to the past to explain the present has other inbuilt problems: memory is notoriously flawed, by the passage of time as well as by the filters on our younger perceptions, which were perceived by a brain not yet capable of abstract, reflective thought. What we recall not only has marginal accuracy, it also doesn't take into account the fact that seeds of awak-

ening like empathy and abiding concern for others require cultivatio
even if they are inherent. This means that we saw things through the ey
of a child not yet capable of adult compassion.

I once learned a technique called Naikan, which originated within Pure
Land Buddhism. Significant childhood events are revisited, and an effort
is made to experience them through the eyes of our caretakers at the time.
There are many limitations, yet it was the first time I'd reflected on the
obvious: that the other people in my life had perceptions that differed
greatly from mine. I remembered mainly my calamities, yet others too
were going through very hard times. Waves of sorrow slowly swept away
long-held resentments. This in turn reinforced my understanding that the
path of unconditioning must be ongoing.

A personal example of the energy behind our ego fortification is that I
spent many years and lots of money on a broad compendium of therapeutic modalities. Finding much of value, I persisted in telling sympathetic
counselors that "if my father had been warmer, my love relationships
would have gone better." Imagine my chagrin when a burst of unsolicited
recall wiped out a host of cherished memories. It was confirmed that I was
the one who had started the battle with my father. My mother described
our first meeting, when I was eighteen months old and he deplaned, returning from World War II. He literally didn't "match my pictures," being a
hundred pounds lighter than the picture I carried everywhere, with skin
and eyes mottled yellow and black from jaundice, malaria, and amoebic
dysentery—which he got after eating raw pig to survive the fifth time one
of the planes he piloted was shot down in the North African desert. My
mother seemed very interested in this creature. I shrieked until I passed
out, with unbudgeable vitriol that didn't stop for two weeks. My father also
had what is now called post-traumatic stress disorder, so it's no surprise

that after two weeks he told my mother, "It's nice to be a father, but do we have to take her everywhere?"

Undeniably, painful things have happened. Still, no one force-fed our reactions to us. The rage of screaming infants and the tantrums and inconsolable grief at the sandbox make it plain that tiny tots come equipped with extreme emotional volatility.

Regardless of our circumstances, the major factor that has a continuing influence on us is the *decisions* we made about events, even more than the events themselves. We don't have to mine the past to discover what these decisions are, since the major ones are still up and running. After moving thirty-five times before age twelve, some of my decisions were: keep your own counsel, don't show feelings, and avoid getting too close to people. Another child might have become clingy. At age four, I made a doozy of a decision: since Daddy seemed to enjoy our banter, if I talked a lot and sounded smart, I would keep him from leaving again. Half a century later, I still talk a blue streak. In fact when my mother heard that I went to a weeklong silent retreat, she said, "*You?* A miracle!"

We may be driven at some point to *decide* that waking up from this bad dream is our only feasible option. In my case, zen has been a providential court of last resort, yet there's much of value in other approaches. As Ezra puts it, "Psychology helps show us what makes us tick; zen helps show us that what makes us tick isn't us." One of the big challenges I've faced has been the desire to develop a "zen ego" to supplant the erosion of my old model.

There we have it: a half-baked recipe for a self.

There's no need to try to move outside the stifling confines of the box we've gotten into; that would just be a change of address. Rather, we can inspect the ego's dimensions and components as thoroughly as we would investigate a diamond, seeing the facets as clearly and objectively as possible, along with whatever dust and fingerprints obscure the brilliance. As awareness cleanses our perception, we find that nature, nurture, and neurosis reflect our true nature, like the facets of a diamond, reflecting everything.

Grow Up, Wake Up: Maturity Levels

Growing up is essential to waking up. Peter Tosh and Bob Marley's reggae civil rights anthem, "Get Up, Stand Up," becomes an anthem of awakening if we change a few words: grow up, wake up . . . wake up from the dream. Most so-called grownups aren't necessarily so grown up, and even if we've been swallowed whole periodically by Aha! moments, our trained parrot won't let tastes of unconditioned reality silence it for long.

In my early years of practice, since zen was big on poems, the first time the walls of my ego took a tumble I wrote this one: Roses are red, violets are blue; two is one, and one is two. It's not Auden, but it points to the absolute nature of relative reality. Shortly thereafter the light dimmed before it illuminated some of my childish ego trips. This called for a second poem: Roses are red, violets are blue; I'm immature, and I am too.

Now that we've considered the anatomy of our ego, let's relate it to maturity levels. As old self-contenders reemerge predictably, we see a Rashomon-like phenomenon: we look like a whole dysfunctional family, all by ourself.

The maturity levels listed here don't reflect developmental phases; they're characteristics sometimes adopted by spiritual practitioners. See which categories ring true for you most often and which come along situationally, such as being adult at work and adolescent on vacations.

Categories overlap somewhat with the Many Me's inventory, since our identity revolves around maturity factors:

- *Infant.* Hysterical, overwhelmed, prone to tantrums or inconsolability.
- *Child.* Needy, clingy, dependency oriented, convinced that others must meet our needs, deferential toward authority figures.
- *Adolescent.* Ambivalent toward authorities, alternatively rebellious and compliant, susceptible to peer pressure, passive-aggressive or aggressive, blasé, yes-butting, or cynical.
- *Parent.* Authoritarian, caretaker, perfectionistic or imperfectionistic in finding fault and trying to fix things, attendant to the needs of others, perhaps claiming to have no personal needs, advise others "for their own good."
- *Adult.* Responsible, values self and others equally, team member or leader, as appropriate. Falls short of wakefulness in that the full-empty dimension isn't conscious, so our identity is still largely confined to me-and-mine.
- *Elder.* Refers to those instants in which the full-empty wonder of things is revealed, allowing the love and inter-being of our nature to shine forth.

Only in the elder maturity level are our perceptions aligned with the fullness of reality. Spiritual aspirants sometimes take on the mask of *pseudo elder,* that is, trying to seem more awake than is the case. Probably some of us have posed as spiritual doctoral candidates when our level of wakefulness was closer to junior high.

The New Testament's I Corinthians verse 13 says "When I was a child, I understood as a child and thought as a child, but when I became a man, I put away childish things." But not always. Truth in packaging requires most of us, at times, to wear "Child on Board" signs sometimes seen in car windows.

While children often demonstrate marvelous attributes, like curiosity, playfulness, and joy, they can hardly be awake, since there hasn't been a chance for seeds of awakening like compassion, loving-kindness, empathic goodwill, discernment, and clear seeing to blossom. The things we admire most in children are also characteristics of older people who have made the acquaintance of unimpeded being.

If we aspire to live an increasingly awake life, our mandate is to grow up. Meantime, we can stay alert to our shifting maturity levels. It's hard to take yourself too seriously when you watch yourself switch abruptly from a childish "Pick me up" stance to an adolescent "Put me down," switching from a needy, dependent "Tell me what to do" demeanor to a foot-stamping "Don't you tell me what to do!"

Maturity levels don't explain everything, yet they are particularly helpful in nurturing the seed of *intrapersonal awareness,* seeing our ego systems objectively. We don't want our gravestone to read "She was like a two-year-old on a bad day and a three-year-old on a good day."

It's inspiring to see signs of spiritual maturity. One morning I drove past Christ the King Church, and the black Christ statue outside the church had been vandalized. By that afternoon someone had put a sign in the statue's broken arms: "Whose hands will you put here?"

12 *The Default Setting*

CONCOCTING THE
SAME OLD "SELF"

When the ego struts its stuff, we don't think that we're enough.
M. T. HEAD, HIPHOP HEART SUTRA

I N   M Y   L A T E   T W E N T I E S, I was asked to give a presentation on a subject I thought I knew a lot about. The topic was conceptual, and halfway through, a voice shot through my head: "What you're saying is all theoretical and won't benefit anyone's life." Whether this was the voice of existential humility or of integrity, just as I was about to tell the participants to pack it in, up came a counteroffer from the ego: "Why not just finish up, and then never, never do this again?"

The self-image that had agreed to do this presentation was a *default setting,* a seemingly hard-wired program that people and compu[,] vert to when the microchips are down. My default setting was to aᵣ knowledgeable, charming, and charismatic. I didn't see what I was doing, since a default setting is closer than our own skin. Familiarity allows it to run with impunity, reinforcing familiar icons. We rarely see it as a fabrication, or rather as a prefabrication, since it's nothing new if we're over two.

You know your default setting is running when you say "That's just the way I am," or "I'm not that kind of person." Defaults differ; one person heads for depression, another for Las Vegas. We approach life reactively— from conditioned ego patterns—rather than responsively, appropriate to a specific situation. Flexibility hardens into rigidity, as our default setting scans like radar for evidence to reinforce its misperceptions.

Greek-Armenian teacher Georges I. Gurdjieff used the term *chief feature* to describe the default setting, a characteristic that could serve life beneficially or reinforce unconsciousness. A default setting comes under the heading of *conditioning,* a term used in spiritual and therapeutic traditions, or *programming,* a term applied to both people and computers (and parrots). It's easy to spot someone else's programming, while our own can be hidden in plain sight, at least from us, particularly if our default happens to be culturally acceptable. For example, one of my default settings has been to buzz around, packing in seemingly noble projects, at times a cover-up to prevent being unmasked as ignoble.

Variations on the default setting abound: anguish addict, confusion junkie, naysayer, top dog, fault-finder, know-it-all, stoic, and catastrophizer. Do you know yours? Our stock phrases provide hints: "Nobody tells me what to do"; "I'm more sensitive than most." Coping strategies also provide clues: to please? withdraw? be aggressive? procrastinate? seek distraction through substances or activity?

Default settings resemble viruses, or rather retroviruses, in the way they seem to skew into our cells and co-opt our life force for their survival. With computers, the solution is simple: install an antivirus program. On the wakeup path, however, our objective isn't to delete something but to become aware of programming that is already running.

Investigating our default setting employs tools from all five dimensions of heartmind. Let's say you're with a new acquaintance you would like to have think highly of you, and you suspect that your automatic-pilot self-images are trying to take over. Take a moment to feel the sensations and movements through which your default setting is strutting its stuff (physical dimension). Listen to the thoughts that are proposing an image to convey (mental dimension). Check to see if habitual mind states are running (emotional dimension). Take a moment to focus on your surroundings (open dimension).

Check-ins like this might be the zen equivalent of defragging a hard disk: available space that we had lost sight of opens up, and our trained parrot's fragmented files, the very things blocking awareness of spaciousness, can't run with the same abandon. Five-dimension awareness like this can be an intense reminder of how unsatisfying a default setting really is.

Bad Me: The Secret Self

Have you seen those Janus-faced masks that are sad on one side and happy on the other? Their two-sidedness reflects two familiar players in our ego drama: our positive persona, the face we try to present to the world, and the flip side, or *bad me*, fraught with inadequacy and kept largely out of sight.

As toddlers, we didn't automatically assume that naughty behavior made us "bad." Caught in the act, we would say "my bad," the answer when someone asks who put the five half-eaten chocolates back in the box. Later we move from "my bad" to bad me, after concluding that doing something bad makes us bad to the bone.

If you think bad me doesn't apply to you, answer this question quickly, before your positive persona takes over: "If people could see the deepest, most painful thing about me, they'd see that I'm utterly . . . fill in the blank: stupid, incompetent, inadequate, flawed, fraudulent, unlovable, hopeless, or useless.

All of them are variations on unworthiness. There's often a correlation between our version of bad me and our positive persona; could there be a connection between my childhood belief that I was stupid and pursuing three academic degrees and becoming a college professor? If we aren't trying to cover something up, what could motivate us to concoct an artificial persona, as opposed to simply doing our best?

Once we suspect that bad me might be at the bedrock of our being, we develop ways to hide it, from seeking approval to seeking comfort in some strange ways. But let a snide comment come our way, and up roars the Unbearable Badness of Being.

Whatever factors contribute to bad me's etiology, the main thing we need to do is to be aware of it, or it will run inaudibly—unless we're thoroughly awake (unlikely) or completely repressed (possibly). We might be shocked to discover an almost perverse attachment to bad me. Sometimes this takes the form of preventive suffering, a self-punishing attitude: "If I beat up on myself, it won't hurt as much when others do it." Don't write this off before seeing whether you can recall a time when you've known that a particular habit, attitude, self-image, or relationship was destructive but continued it anyway.

DIS—Discovering Your Bad Me: A Worksheet

"DIS," shorthand for "disrespect" in the neighborhood, is an acronym for decisions (D), image (I), and strategies (S), the components of bad me. Fill in your version.

D for decisions. What conclusions have you made about being unacceptable? ("If I get close to people, they'll see that I'll never measure up.")

I for image. How do you fear people will see you? Picture a Polaroid snapshot of bad me's facial expression and bodily posture. Notice how it differs from your positive persona.

S for strategies. What are your game plans for keeping bad me out of sight? They might be conventionally appropriate, like doing good things to hide presumed inadequacies, or inappropriate, like engaging in harmful activities or purposely conveying an incompetent image.

As we increase our awareness of the ways we DIS ourselves, they will be less likely to go latent and emerge periodically to undermine things. We can stay alert to the bodily tension that signals that bad me is imprisoned, under the lockdown of tight muscles. Looking around, we can see this chronic armoring even in small children, who have no better solution for dealing with pain. And we are those children, all grown up.

Fortunately, bad me can't be the real us, nor can our positive persona, if we consider the rapidity with which both can show up or disappear at the drop of a criticism or compliment. This is a powerful

lesson in impermanence, the lack of any solid or abiding self, certainl
not a bad one.

Lemon Meringue "I": Living Outside the Pie

We've already discovered how perplexing ego identities can be, given that there's multiplicity where we expected unity. The Lemon Meringue "I" pie analogy shows how three of our major identity layers intermesh and shift, sometimes in rapid succession. To make the analogy pertinent, think of a relationship or situation that has had some ups and downs. Recall a time when you were at your best: pleasing, competent, on top of things, whatever. This is the *meringue*, the facade we hope others will buy. In less conscious moments, we may buy it ourselves.

Now bite down to the bottom of the pie, and you find the *soggy crust*. This layer surfaces when we've been overturned by rejection or a bad me attack. The soggy crust is the low point of our game.

The third layer, the *sour filling*, may not show up until after we've endured some bounces between the meringue and the soggy crust. Like the meringue, it serves to keep our soggy crust out of sight. The sour filling's motto is "If life gives you lemons, suck 'em!" Sour flavors include resentful, untrusting, coolly cynical, hardhearted, passive-aggressive, world-weary, and blaming. People often retreat into the sour filling increasingly as they age.

People deal differently with these layers of ego identity. Some struggle to keep the meringue intact, which guarantees stiff artificiality. Others take up a steady diet of sour lemons. Some plummet readily into the soggy crust and anguished despair.

We'd never be driven to concoct a drippy meringue or to take refuge in the sour filling's bitterness if we weren't convinced deep down that the soggy crust is the awful truth about us. However, these seemingly indigestible layers can start to break down when we approach them the same way we would approach an actual pie: ingest and digest. Ingesting starts by acknowledging what's really on our plate, stiff, sweet, tart, or soggy. Then the digestive enzyme of awareness can do its job: physically, we feel quivers and scrunched-up sensations; mentally, we note our mind's running commentary; and emotionally, we see what mood or tone predominates. The open awareness dimension, via our surroundings, serves as a plate for our pie.

Observation shows how futile it is to try to create a solid self out of components that are inconsistent, incomplete, and insubstantial.

13 *Loving-Kindness*
A MEDITATION

What might it be like to awaken each day into an increasing sense that being loving is even more important than being loved?
STEPHEN LEVINE

A HUNGARIAN Orthodox rabbi in prison at Auschwitz was being led to the gas chamber. He thanked the guards for their kindness and said, "Today, my friends, I will meet Ha Shem [The Name]," and danced his way to extermination. I heard this from my friend Rabbi Mary Jane Newman, who learned of it from the rabbi's grandson.

This story touches a spot similar to that of Jacques Luysseran, a blind French Resistance detainee, who describes gratitude at being privileged to encourage his comrades, even though they stole his bread in the Buchenwald Concentration Camp.*

I don't know what led these men in the direction of love and kindness, but I know of no practice more valuable for contacting the indestructible—even in destructive circumstances—than the Loving-Kindness meditation, described by the Buddha and practiced in different spiritual traditions.

The four lines of the meditation outline the interweaving trajectory of a spiritual life: inviting loving-kindness to awaken, attending to whatever blocks loving-kindness, opening to the fullness of the moment, and extending the wish that all existence be pervaded by loving-kindness.

Loving-Kindness: The Meditation

Let the body settle. Close your eyes as attention turns to the sensation of breathing, in the palpitating chest center. Placing several fingertips there helps to attune awareness.

On an inhalation, picture or sense someone you care for, even a pet, just to get the juices of goodwill flowing. Breathe their image into the center of your chest, and on the outbreath silently say, "May loving-kindness awaken," extending your wish for their well-being. Now envision yourself, on successive inbreaths, with awareness still

* Jacques Luysseran, *And There Was Light: The Autobiography of a Blind Hero of the French Resistance,* trans. Elizabeth Cameron (Sandpoint, Idaho: Morning Light Press, 2000).

centered in the chest, and silenty say the following lines on the exhalations:

1. May loving-kindness awaken.
2. May whatever clouds loving-kindness be attended and healed.
3. May this moment be experienced, just as it is.
4. May loving-kindness extend to all.

Repeat these four lines several times. Then think of someone else you care for and sense their image. Repeat the process with them in mind. On the fourth line, awareness can extend to include those in the immediate vicinity. Next, choose another person and follow the same procedure. Sometimes for other people, the first two lines are sufficient. Finish by reflecting on all beings, repeating the lines, in dedication to this expanded sense of life.

Awareness is fostered by the multisensory form this version of Loving-Kindness takes: *sensing* the pulsating touchpoint of the chest center, *visualizing* the person to whom the meditation is addressed, and *experiencing* the sentience to which each line points. The hub is chest-centered breathing, where the separating emotions, like anger, and the connecting qualities, like empathy and gratitude, often announce themselves. They can be explored firsthand through this meditation.

The word "extending" is similar to formal zen services, which say, "May this compassionate expression be extended to all beings, and may we realize the awakened way together."

The Loving-Kindness meditation accords with zen's Bodhisattva vow, in confirming that our awakening is mutually grounded in the interdependence of all beings, rather than being a self-centered endeavor.

Loving-kindness is sometimes misconstrued as an attempt to conjure up good feelings, or to see ourselves as loving or kind. However, its function is to invite the awakening of compassion and empathy, aspects of our being. Sometimes mind states arise that seem to be the opposite of loving or kindness: on the fourth line, extending loving-kindness to all, you might think, "Wellll, maybe not so and so." If this happens, you can return to the second line and respectfully include any strong thoughts or feelings in experiential awareness.

Sometimes warmth, benign friendliness, goodwill, tolerance, or energy arises. If so, on an exhalation, this can be extended to a person or throughout your body or surroundings.

The wording can be modified, provided the essence isn't altered. Changing words periodically revitalizes our view, so don't hesitate to substitute words like *compassion, heartmind,* or *empathic goodwill* for loving-kindness; all are seeds of awakening.

There is no "I" in the wording here; it doesn't require a self for loving-kindness to arise.

If we have ever wished that we could have marinated in loving-kindness, we don't have to wait any longer. Loving-kindness can reveal that we are never alone, the understanding that underlies love.

When Loving-Kindness is addressed to those in distress or without a spiritual path, the second line might read, "May you be healed in your suffering" or "May you be free from unnecessary suffering" to express our wish that unavoidable pain not be exacerbated by painful emotional reactions. When we include people with whom we have unresolved grievances, it may be sufficient to use only the second line for the time being.

The version of Loving-Kindness above uses the word "may" to acknowledge the deep wish for heartmind to awaken. Next we have a shorthand version that presupposes some practice with the first one. The lines here are reduced to a single word, to minimize language. The instructions are the same as above.

1. Awakening (loving-kindness).
2. Attending (whatever clouds loving-kindness).
3. Experiencing (this moment).
4. Extending (loving-kindness to all).

More important than words is whether the Loving-Kindness meditation bears fruit in our lives, through a diminution of sourness and the upwelling of the openness of heartmind.

Don't be surprised if early attempts seem as dry as drawing water from an unused well. First, up comes the sludge of resistance or resentment, then dirty water, our grudging thoughts or self-pity. Finally, the clear water that has been there all along flows forth, and will continue to flow, provided the wellsprings of loving-kindness are visited regularly.

14 The Emotional Dimension Meets Meditation

Zen does not teach to destroy all the impulses, instincts and affective factors that make up the human heart; it only teaches to clear up our intellectual insights from erroneous discrimination and unjustifiable assumptions. For when this is done, the heart knows by itself how to work out its native virtues.

D. T. SUZUKI

DURING MY FIRST YEAR of college teaching, Sylver Miller, a student, came by my office, and she said, "Sometimes your teaching style seems like a platitudinous elaboration of the insignificantly obvious." My stomach plummeted, but I smiled politely. Before leaving, she said with a chipper grin, "You really can spout those veritable truisms. See ya!"

After the semester ended, knowing my love of birds, she gave me a cockatiel that someone had given her husband, who didn't like birds. I was thrilled with the prospect of having Pepito, but he immediately bonded with my then husband, who was completely indifferent to him. I, on the other hand, adored Pepito and tried my best to ingratiate myself, but he couldn't stand me. This was a crash course in zen's three delusions: *attachment, aversion,* and *indifference* (unawareness or ignore-ance). We all know how they work: when the me magnet wants something and tries to pull it in, that's attachment. When the me magnet reverses is poles and tries to repel something, that's aversion. When we consider something unworthy of attention, that's indifference. These three delusions are staples in the emotional diet of our trained parrot.

Before we continue, here's the working definition we will use for "emotion": an amalgam of strongly believed thoughts, intense bodily sensations, and a forcefully held notion of "me." We'll keep our focus on the internal components of emotions and regard the words, actions, and interactions that issue forth from the emotion as expressions, rather than as being technically part of the emotion.

There's not much information on the emotional travails of well-known historical spiritual figures. This seems odd, when you consider that emotions are one of the primary fruits of the womb of ego. Neither is much said about how to practice directly with emotional upheaval, to my knowledge. I'm grateful to two eighteenth-century Japanese adepts, Menzan Zuiho Zenji and Hakuin Ekaku Zenji, for bringing emotions out of the closet. Menzan Zenji sums things up beautifully: "If you think that you have cut off illusory thoughts, instead of clarifying how emotion-thought melts, the emotion-thought will come up again, as though you had cut off the stem of a blade of grass or the trunk of a tree and left the root alive."*

* Menzan Zuiho Zenji, in *Shikan Taza,* ed. and trans. Shohaku Okumura (Kyoto: Kyoto Soto-Zen Publications, 1985).

Hakuin discussed his own physical and emotional symptoms in the autobiographical "Yasenkanna."* When he was at the apex of the Zen Buddhist world, he humbly sought assistance in an attempt to correct apparent imbalances following many years of austerities. It's encouraging to learn about someone of his stature who willingly acknowledged that suffering in the various dimensions of heartmind can occur at any point in our practice.

Zen practice has to illuminate the agonies that otherwise obscure the ecstasy. At my first sesshin, Soen Roshi proved his adroitness at this when I threw a small fit during our first interview. The retreat was held during a 103-degree heat wave, with twenty-five women sleeping on the floor of a flea-infested room. You had to choose between brushing your teeth or using the toilet before dawn sitting, and I opted for the toilet. I was soon thrust into Soen Roshi's interview room in the grips of a mortified snit over having halitosis when meeting the Great Zen Master. Soen Roshi improvised a lesson on how to brush my teeth with my fingers and asked how I had slept. Fine. Beaming, he gave me a koan and sent me on my way. He had held up a compassionate mirror to the fact that after getting a good night's sleep, I'd been practically undone by a tiny thing. After sesshin, he gave me the spotless napkin he had used for every meal that week, saying gently, "We try not to make too big a mess." I still have that napkin, as a reminder to contain emotional spills within the napkin of practice.

Practice isn't about eradicating emotions. Yet as a Japanese proverb says, "Every little yielding to anxiety is a step away from the natural heart of man."† Note, it doesn't say anxiety is the problem; it's the yielding to

* Trevor Leggett, *The Tiger's Cave* (London: Routledge & Kegan Paul, 1977).
† M. Strauss, ed. *Familiar Medical Quotations* (Boston: Little, Brown, 1968).

anxiety that takes us afield. Fortunately, awareness heals; still, we'd better fasten our seat belts, since the ride can get wild and woolly.

Mind States Up Close: A Worksheet

The Sanskrit term *duhkha* refers to a wheel that is out of kilter and doesn't go around smoothly—the way we react when the separating emotions are stirred up. Let's see what's already amassed in the spice rack of our emotional pantry.

Circle the srongest traits that you are likely to exhibit. Add words to any category as you like.

If you want to start applying your newfound knowledge in your daily-life practice, keep tabs on the items you marked. You can check to see how they show up in your relationships, workplace, and family events.

The items listed here are grouped by categories that reflect similarities.

- *Attachment.* Needy, needy-greedy, grasping, clinging.
- *Aversion* (also see "anger"). Reluctant, fearful, frozen, doubtful, contemptuous, heedless, withdrawn, jealous, envious.
- *Indifferent.* Spaced out, ignorant, in fantasyland, avoiding, pseudo-detached, "not here," negligent.
- *Agitated.* Restless, anxious, jangled, stressed.
- *Angry.* A hothead, irritable, blaming, aggressive, grumpy, critical, carrying a chip on my shoulder, rebellious, a bully, frustrated,

resentful, complaining, passive-aggressive, a martyr, a victim, contemptuous, self-righteous, indignant, bitter, self-pitying, contentious, envious, defensive, cynical, easily hurt, arrogant, competitive, confrontational, a grievance collector, revengeful, sarcastic.

- *Compliant.* Pleasing, a yes-person, a goody-goody, respectful, polite, empathic.
- *Depressed.* Melancholy, hopeless, despairing, desperate.
- *Doubtful.* Confused, indecisive, iffy, yes-butting.
- *Fearful.* Panicked, anxious, worried, terrified, timid, paranoid, overwhelmed.
- *Grief-stricken, sad.* Anguished, lost, suffering, disappointed, hurt.
- *In charge.* Aggressive, bossy, arrogant, a know-it-all, in control, on top of it all, competitive, rebellious.
- *Numb.* Frozen, in denial, dead to the world.
- *Special.* Unique, superior, misunderstood, different, proud, arrogant, overly sensitive, contemptuous, an exception to the rules, a prisoner of moods.
- *Upbeat.* Cheerful, on top of it, nicey-nice, a people pleaser, stoic.
- *Other.* Pathetic, inadequate, obsessive, funny, cute, fill in the blank.

Emotions as a Path of Awakening: Clarifying Actions, Interactions, and Reactions

It's possible to feel several emotions at once, as I discovered in the midst of a duo-harpsichord concert with Igor Kipnis. As we reached the last page of a Bach concerto, the fire alarm in the auditorium went off. Igor and I peeked at each other and kept going, finishing the last fifteen seconds of the piece just as the alarm stopped wailing. Igor turned nonchalantly to the audience and said, "Is that anything we need to worry about?" Then he told the audience that he'd actually been panicked and had only kept going because he thought I looked so focused. The audience was delighted, probably having assumed that a Grammy-winning artist would be beyond distractibility or panic during a performance. Later we laughed over our kaleidoscopically shifting emotions: delight in the music, fright over the fire alarm, and relief that no one was in imminent danger.

It's encouraging when someone well known admits to being susceptible to emotions, since it makes it easier for others to admit to being affected. Emotions are a pandemic, from supermarket checkout lines to social conversations that resemble a talk show format: one minute to raise the topic and fifty minutes for emotions and opinions to fly. We can see the importance of addressing them directly as a component of formal spiritual practice. Wouldn't it be fascinating if monitors were installed on the foreheads of meditators, broadcasting the drama that can run during still, outwardly silent sittings? It might resemble a cross between a soap opera and *The Twilight Zone.*

Most of us have a consistent, well-rehearsed strategy for dealing with emotions, falling into the following categories:

Stuff it. Denial. "Oh, I don't get upset; I'm a meditator." Stuffers may not know they're upset. Asked whether or not they're angry, they might say, "Oh, I'm not angry. People just aren't doing what they should." Another version of denial involves being quite aware of our emotions but keeping them under wraps. Some spiritual circles place a premium on the appearance of transcendence, but it's highly unlikely that emotionality has been transformed, unless we've been to hell and back. Even if you forget about it, it's there.

Think our emotions. Mentally recycling emotional tape loops. The assumption is that if emotions aren't verbalized, then no harm done, right? Wrong. Mental wallowing not only entrenches our reactive ruts, it's communicable.

Talk about emotions. Verbal regurgitation of our stew, through gossip, whining, complaint, or blame. We make our case, trying to convince others that our position is correct, expressing upsets as facts of life: "I just want to share with you, out of love, *that you . . . ruined . . . my . . . life!!!*" We're not talking here about consultations intended to clarify emotional reactions. Some counseling and communication modalities can be effective, provided we refrain from repetitive emoting or sympathy seeking. While it's understandable to want to be comforted, learning to differentiate between sympathy and genuine empathy is a key part of emotional clarification.

Act out emotions. Gestures, hitting, kicking, stomping, throwing, and yelling, where the use of tone, vocabulary, and body language become weapons. All of the things listed here are actions, not emotions. People who act out may believe that they're in touch with their emotions, but that's unlikely. Acting out veers close to suppression, with the same limited awareness of bodily sensation, or even the locale. It isn't called "blind rage" for nothing: "I didn't think. I just saw red, and the next thing I knew, he was lying on the ground." There may be witnesses, but there's no *witness*.

Whether we are stuffers or dumpers, there are consequences to emotional mismanagement. Stuffing exacerbates contents under pressure, as in the cliché: "He was such a good boy, so quiet—until he started shooting." Dumping can be internal—thinking our emotions—or external, talking or acting our emotions. Either way, the results qualify as a toxic waste site.

There's a fifth approach, in which we have almost no training:

Experience emotions. This involves feeling the physiological components that accompany our emotional story line—the heavy chest and collapsed posture. This category is the only option where bodily feelings are consciously felt, and feelings are meant to be felt, by definition. Many of us are equipped with a bodily barometer—the head, chest, or stomach—that portends impending stormy weather.

When people first hear about *experiencing,* it can be confused with emotional repression, particularly if we have received messages conveying a mandate not to feel: "If you keep crying, I'll give you something to cry about." In the wake of such messages, we might conclude that showing, or even having, feelings is potentially dangerous.

In no way does the experiencing option imply rolling over and playing dead. The point is to allow our emotions to come alive viscerally, backlit by environmental awareness. Still dubious? The next time a strong emotion arises, see if you can really maintain any sort of planetary awareness or inner bodily sensation if you hop immediately into externalizing the emotion.

Even after we think we know a lot about our emotions, reactivity can resurface precipitously. Recently, a fairly new meditation practitioner was in the hospital for surgery and became so agitated that the nurse asked, "Have you ever considered meditation?"

Frequent over-the-edge moments are a neon sign, indicating the need to pay more attention to emotivity. Otherwise, more pain will be generated and passed along. The next time your emotions are running high, answer the following questions, on a scale of one to ten (ten is high):

1. To what extent do I believe that my emotional reaction is the most significant part of the issue, and that I'm thereby justified in indulging it?
2. How much is my ego identity fortified by my reaction? Which identity?
3. How willing am I to practice with my reaction, rather than indulge it?
4. How clearly do I know what specific practice approaches for dealing with upsets would be helpful, and how willing am I to engage in the process?

Don't be surprised if the answers are (1) ten, (2) eleven, (3) one, and (4) zero and no!

As we head for the roots of the emotional dimension, the resulting decompression shows that our leaden reactivity is gold at the core.

Reactions Revisited—Action, Interaction, Reaction: A Meditation

If emotional upsets come up when we're in the middle of a task or others are present, it's better to wait than to blurt.

Reactions Revisited makes it possible to stow our reaction, providing a template for revisiting the situation later. If we do tuck a reaction away, we'll definitely need to get back to it for an awareness session later, or it's likely to rumble around inside building up steam instead of revealing its full-empty aggregates. Reactions Revisited is a skillful use of memory, a way to recall a situation and look at and feel the conditioning that has been running just below our facade. After each item, close your eyes in order to feel and hear what the line evokes.

1. Recall the trigger. Recall the situation as vividly as possible for a few breaths. Get carried away with your feelings about it, as if you're not a spiritual type. Picture or remember what happened and who was involved.

2. Recall the mental components. Briefly recall the following:

- What was said?
- What did you think?
- What was most disheartening?
- Is it a familiar theme?
- How have you been told to act or think in such situations?
- What did you want to say?
- What did you say?
- What strong opinions are still reverberating from the situation?
- What is your most believed thought about the situation, the thing you find most painful or frightening about all of this?
- What was said or done that was most bothersome, or most painful to your identity?

3. Recall your emotional and mind states. Recall how you felt—mad, sad, scared, or other?

4. Let attention turn to bodily awareness. Let your thoughts recede to *call waiting.*

5. Feel your bodily sensations. Feel your strongest physical sensations for about three breaths. If sensations are evasive, find the area where there seems to be the most numbness. If nothing seems to stand out, pick your torso or chest, since your breathing and heartbeat can be felt there.

If sensations flit away once again, recall the situation momentarily so your reaction can return, and then check again for sensations. If physical sensations have been long unwelcome, they fear coming out of deep freeze.

6. Optional: Trigger phrase, let your sensations speak. When a strong sensation arises, you might ask, "Is there anything this sensation would like to say?" There might be a trigger word that describes your sensations viscerally: sinking, shrinking, cringing, shaking, contracting; then, whether a trigger phrase or word comes blurting out or nothing comes up, return to sensations and proceed.

7. Breathe. Include your strongest sensations as an accompaniment to your breathing, feeling how they intermingle.

8. Oscillate between sensations and surroundings. Let the field of environmental sounds and space around you encompass sensations.

9. Practice presence. Resume your responsibilities with as much awareness as possible.

If residual unpleasant feelings remain, acknowledge that they can come up later for further visits, as necessary. With ongoing practice, bodily sensations will become accustomed to being aerated by the sensations of breathing, and this exercise can be folded into daily life.

Reactions Revisited will probably get lots of workouts, since life keeps bringing up old reactions to situations. You can use just the trigger phrase to evoke repeats. Regular practice makes it possible to greet formerly frustrating situations with curiosity, and even kindness.

15 *Anger and Fear*

When anger is blazing, instead of throwing kerosene on it, try extending heartmind.

M. T. HEAD

A FTER LOSING A RUN-IN with an adult at age three, I made
a decision: anger is off limits. From that time on, I kept my anger
largely under the rug, only to have it erupt thirty years later, when I was still
fairly new to zen practice. What goes down must come up, and the lockdown on anger had only succeeded in putting off the inevitable. No longer
could it be denied: anger must be addressed specifically, within the auspices
of spiritual practice. I've always been grateful to Ram Dass for telling us,
one summer when I had an opportunity to spend three months with him,
that he had realized that what he had formerly considered "dharmic anger"
was just plain anger.

Those drawn to zen are likely to keep anger in check, at least outwardly; but friends and family may see another side. We may pride ourselves on not getting angry yet be prone to complaining, blaming, whining, feeling sorry for ourselves, road rage, or reciting grievances to virtual strangers—all of which belong to the anger family's sliding scale from frustration to fury. No one is exempt from anger's thrall. We don't need a clinical diagnosis to know the extent to which diminished capacity sets in when anger takes over.

If anger is aboard, we need to know about it. This isn't as straightforward as it sounds, though, given that for some people, early childhood was anger's last stand, at least overtly. The terrible twos failed to establish us as the boss of the world, and we probably received early messages on anger mismanagement—like being smacked for smacking another child, reinforcing exactly what the adult was trying to prevent.

Anger's stew is thickened by religious and educational injunctions not to show anger, often gender based: "Good girls don't get angry" or "Boys can show anger to other boys, but not around the house." One of the most unfortunate messages surrounding anger is "You've made me very angry," implying that others are responsible for our emotions. This common assumption fortifies a disempowering victim stance, and those who are angered don't have to take responsibility for their emotional condition. If that were true, children might be the most powerful family members, capable of controlling the emotional state of adults by acting up. Think about it: if you see an adult brutalizing a small child at a Laundromat, do you have to get angry?

All you really need to do is to get help to stop the situation in the most beneficial way; getting angry usually doubles the trouble. Many of us have an invisible residue of unfinished emotional business stowed away, simmering like volcanic lava under an apparently calm surface. This may not be apparent until there's been some slip in the success of our tactics for handling anger: control it, project it, redirect it, reject it, or eject it. When these fail to produce the peace we desire down deep, we may turn to spirituality in hopes of finding imperturbability. While it's true that equanimity tends to grow through meticulous practice, we shouldn't minimize the challenge involved.

Sometimes anger is dismissed as delusion, to be eradicated through meditation or special states. Tales may be told about spiritual beings who have transcended anger—always long ago and far away. The antidote for this is found in cautionary tales like the one about a zen hermit, admired for being beyond anger. One day in the market he saw a squash he wanted, and when someone else reached for it, the anger-free hermit grabbed it and hit him with it!

If we try to bypass dealing directly with anger, we'll be ill prepared when anger starts to come out sideways, take on steamroller tendencies, or eat us alive from the inside. Construing zen precepts concerning anger to mean that angry thoughts and feelings should never arise is also a misunderstanding. We can, however, learn to recognize the signs of anger brewing and refrain from dramatizing it.

Anger and Awakening

When anger arises, here's a quick mantra: shut your mouth. At the very least, this curtails the ejection of anger through yelling, blaming, or verbal violence—all of which are unjustified. One way to buy precious awareness moments is to say, "Let me get back to you on that." Far from being wishy-washy or backing down, this is central to diplomacy, and it provides an interval during which more harmonious alternatives might occur to us.

Have you ever noticed that people sometimes behave better when playing games than in "real life," with occasional exceptions in professional athletes or little league parents? Maybe people intend to enjoy themselves at games. Also, games have quite a few tools for slowing down the rush of anger, such as rules, fouls, team captains, coaches, referees, and time-outs.

Time-outs are tremendously helpful, for adults as well as for sporting types and kids, particularly when anger flares. We may see the value, in principle, but there's little follow-through when time-outs are most needed. Why? Because *when we're angry we almost never think we're wrong.* This is doubly true for those of us who are recovering doormats, who have long kept anger in check and can experience an almost irresistible urge to rise up: "Never again will anyone sideline me when I'm upset!" At such times, no matter how much training we have in conscious communication and empathic listening, we may be shocked to find that just when we need these tools most, we're rolling like a runaway truck. Fueled by internally produced adrenal steroids, we may find we have little interest in communicating consciously.

Never underestimate the addictive quality of anger. Unlike drugs and mind-altering substances, which are ingested into the body, the chemicals that fuel anger are manufactured within the body and mind, even if events trigger the reaction. Anyone who has a strong proclivity toward anger needs to understand that indulging in it is equivalent to an alcoholic going on a drinking binge.

Another thing we need to emphasize is the inaccuracy of a common assumption that people can't, or won't, take action unless they're angry.

The flaw in this is seen when considering the impact of Rosa Parks, Aung San Suu Kyi, Gandhi, Thich Nhat Hanh, and Dr. Martin Luther King; all of these people have brought about constructive changes in the world without resorting to anger-driven utterances or acts. These people developed the capacity to differentiate between the issues, on the one hand, and their emotional reactions to the issues, on the other. We can too. Their ability to focus on issues rather than reactions has dignified their efforts to heal prejudice, colonialism, hunger, inequality, and terrorism. I have personally heard Rosa Parks and Thich Nhat Hanh speak of the need to encounter anger in the solitude of spiritual practice.

The next time we think something is "infuriating," we might want to stop and feel into our reaction and then ask, "What's the most constructive thing that I can do without demonstrating anger in the process?" And then we bring awareness to the components of anger, as part of meditation.

It's no wonder anger seems to practically rule the world. We may not be motivated to investigate its tentacles until we can no longer overlook the misery caused by our own anger. When that time comes, we'll be fortunate to be able to differentiate between the *situation*, the *reaction*, and the *practice tools* that assist us in awakening within anger. This in turn enables our words and actions to become more powerful and harmonious and less divisive.

As our anger begins to dissolve into its elements, we may see why clarifying anger is sometimes considered a straight route to actualizing *resolve*, the seed of awakening that carries the strength of anger but not anger's harmful consequences. Disarmament begins at home.

Anger and Breathing: An Exercise

Physically based practices help us dip into anger's contraction, so that anger can begin to resolve into sheer energy and sensation. Abdominal (*hara* in Japanese, *dantien* in Chinese) breathing approaches are prominent in some martial arts and the Lin Chi (Rinzai in Japanese) zen school. Folk wisdom and some physiological systems credit this area of the body with possessing some degree of savvy in processing anger.

Start by settling into a balanced position, and take a few deep breaths to refresh bodily awareness. For about a minute, let your breathing center in the abdomen, feeling the inflations and deflations.

Then bring to mind a scenario that arouses anger, and fume with abandon for up to one minute. Next, turn to your body's sensations. For several breaths, let awareness trickle down toward your abdomen on each exhalation.

Once your awareness is established in the abdomen, briefly sense the sensations, reaction, and breath contained within a beach ball in your belly, which fills and empties on successive rounds of breathing.

To finish, let your breathing open into the rest of your body. Then awareness opens to include your surroundings, the ground and the sky. This spaciousness has room for the aftermath of your anger and everything else. Repeat as needed.

To intensify the practice you can allow your pelvic floor, the area surrounding the perineum, to contract on exhales, and then release on inhales. Soen Roshi liked to describe the variations involving the pelvic floor, using colorful terms for sphincters. He said that sailors who knew how to do this were less likely to drown if their ship sank. We may not need this application; however, since anger can figuratively sink our ship, this exercise is likely to come in handy.

Fear

Fear is a great solidifier, one of the primary blinders that keep heartmind out of sight. Even if harsh emotions like anger cause more harm in the world, how often is fear a propelling factor? Fear leaves us feeling like a snail without a shell, afraid, defenseless. Isn't it when we feel unprotected that we do all sorts of harmful things?

We shy away from fear; as Hot Lips Hoolihan used to say on *M*A*S*H*, "I don't like fear. It scares me." No wonder, considering how unappealing its masks are: dread, apprehensiveness, alarm, panic attacks, trepidation, worry, cold feet, anxiety, foreboding, and phobias. "Stress," a catchall phrase, is largely populated by fear's kin.

Ironically, as inevitable as fear is, people rarely own up to being afraid. It's unusual to see undisguised fear except in small children, since at a certain age we start covering up our fear by whistling in the dark. We can spew out a barrage of obscurations as opaque as octopus ink, hoping to keep our fear invisible. Thus we may even lose contact with fear's presence, until it catches us off guard.

What do we fear? Almost anything: being devalued, unlovable, out of control, insecure, lonely, or worthless. Some people fear abandonment; as odd as it may sound, I used to fear that people who had stopped loving me would *stay* rather than leave, thus providing constant reminders that I was unlovable!

Our ways of covering fear are innumerable, starting with several "f-word" options: *fight, flee, freeze, fantasize,* and *fake friendliness.* These are reactions that color, or rather discolor, the fear that is already present, adding more pain to our considerable stash. We may try to distract ourselves from our fear by staying busy, trying to avoid the tension and worry that accumulate when we fear that the fear monster is gaining on us. Covering our fear with fearful-looking demeanors may sound strange, but people often avoid even greater fears through addiction to self-doubt, confusion, indecisiveness, and weak or timid demeanors.

Some of fear's camouflages have been considered acceptable parts of gender conditioning, such as the "helpless woman in need of protection" style that was popular when I moved to South Carolina from Utah at age eleven. To my shock, my peers were already adept at using what were then called "feminine wiles" to attract attention as our hormones started to rage. I took off my baseball cap. Even though I was already full to the brim with fear, I hoped to get into the social action—but I couldn't manage to bring off this facade. I chose a different way to hide my fear, striving to become the smartest and most talented seventh grader; maybe, I reasoned, I would be included if I were helpful enough by tutoring or entertaining enough by playing piano for assemblies. This may be hard to imagine, but being onstage in front of the entire student body playing the piano seemed less frightening than facing one of those girls on the playground.

There are also angry-looking cover-ups for fear, like suiting up in the seemingly impenetrable armor of righteous indignation, contrariness, resentment, or belligerence. These may provide a false sense of safety, but they leave us just as uncomfortable as before, compounding the tension of fear with the tensions of anger.

One cloak of fear, sometimes found in spiritual circles, is hiding fear's quiver under the cloak of imperturbability. This eventually starts to feel like the chitin exoskeleton of some insect, brittle and disconnected.

One apparent difference between humans and other animals is that when animals are frightened or startled, they run, thus depleting their buildup of adrenalin. Compliant or withdrawn species tend to remain inactive when frightened. The buildup of cortisol courses through our veins, causing cellular mischief. If we double the impact by mulling over the frightening situation, the stress chemicals are eventually compounded into free-floating anxiety; we're scared, and nothing seems to be causing it. As we sing Muddy Waters's "Worried Life Blues," we project our worries onto whatever seems perilous—that other country, the stock market, politics. Worst of all, when physical danger is actually imminent, the reservoir of our built-up fear may flood, paralyzing us with panic, making us unable to respond. When we're immobilized, the results can be worse that the situation that evoked the fear.

We may reach the point where we even fear happiness, regarding it as a sign that the axe might be about to fall. Yet it's miserable seeing life through a tunnel of fear. So we bring out our basic awareness tools, feeling the unpleasant physical sensations, recognizing the primary thoughts that goad our fear.

A key point in working with fear is to keep asking a fundamental question: "What is this?" The question is *not* "What is this *about*," which leads to historical rehashes. The answer to "what is this" is always physical. For instance, let's say we're afraid a new acquaintance is going to write us off. Rather than withdrawing or turning on the charm, we take a few moments to feel our clenched neck and shaky hands, and stay engaged in whatever is going on.

The components of fear span the physical, mental, and emotional dimensions of heartmind, so the checklists from those sections are useful in unmasking our fear. The open awareness dimension is particularly helpful, providing breathing room for our fear to come out into the open, rather than remaining constricted by the narrowed attention of unaddressed fear.

Entering directly into fear may seem as scary as walking into our apartment late at night and having something brush against our arm. Terror! Turning on the light, we see that our winter scarf on the hook by the door is gently caressing our shoulder. The dim corners of consciousness can seem like this, until we have a closer look. Embracing our fear is part of being one with everything. Unexamined fear starts the cascade of other deadly four-letter words: *fear* to *hate* to calling something we fear *evil*, to a justification to *kill*. Uninterrupted, the cycle mushrooms into hate crimes, religious warfare, and unimaginable atrocities. Fear is the most benign of these four-letter words, and all that it asks is what friends usually ask: that we give the fear some respectful attention and listen compassionately to its voice.

It has been said that fear is the opposite of love. Actually, love, in its fullness, has no opposite and can encompass even fear within its loving circle. By taking the necessary baby steps to experience our fear, we express our wish to live in the openness and wholeheartedness of love.

16 *Disheartenment*

GRAY DAYS AND
DARK NIGHTS

When we understand that there is no stability to be found in life other
than living it out as it is, we will be able to comprehend the reasoning
behind the principle of becoming emancipated from our pain and
suffering by just being resolved to living through it as it is.
KOSHO UCHIYAMA

IF WE HAVEN'T YET encountered the depths of despair, we
might not understand how someone could become depressed just by
looking at the sky on a sunny day or come to regard humanity as a failed
experiment. At such times, we may find petitionary upwellings that harken
back to our childhood religion coming from our lips—"God, help me"—

perhaps addressed to a deity or the unknown or a higher power, or to temporarily unavailable aspects of our total being.

We have to be pretty far down to realize that our ego isn't capable of compassionate attention when our consolations and compensations are falling aside like leaves from a tree in autumn. Self-motivated willpower falls short here.

Disheartenment, the deep end of the emotional dimension, takes us into increasingly painful depths, starting with burnout, where we still see ourselves as having some sense of power, some teeth for biting into life. This contrasts with the increasing sense of helplessness and lifelessness as we descend through dismay, depression, and despair, finally hitting bottom.

Facing and embracing disheartenment seems to be a necessary precondition for empathic living, for truly seeing ourselves in others. It appears that there's no way to avoid what Pema Chödrön calls "the whole stinking mess." It's no wonder that people who have made compassionate contributions to the greater good often allude to encounters with the dark nights of the soul. Knowing that this is part of the path helps us understand why Viktor Frankl felt a sense of responsibility for writing down what he went through in a concentration camp, believing it might help those who are subject to despair. All of us qualify at times.

Formal zen practice has much to offer through the riptides of disheartenment. If our health permits, regular practice with moving meditation forms like chi kung, tai chi, and yoga can be a boon in keeping the body instrument tonified and resilient. Never underestimate the value of intense practice, such as meditation retreats. These stand us in good stead through their paradoxical element of *intentional suffering,* or willingly entering into voluntary discomfort. Far from being masochistic, such encounters provide evidence of our capacity to abide in, and absorb, the inevitable ardors that life serves up. If our spiritual practice doesn't specifically prepare us for encountering a certain degree of difficulty in life, and give a slight push at the edges of our comfort area, we may be left stranded when our need is greatest.

When our particular version of the dark night can no longer be denied, we might consider taking up the koan "In times of disheartenment, what is the best refuge?" Referring back to what we've gleaned in the various dimensions of heartmind and bringing them to bear in gray times may help us discover that the exhale of despair can be followed by an inhale of wonder and appreciation.

Burnout and Burning Aspiration

Sometimes aspiration burns brightly. Abounding with life's flow, we're eager to share our enthusiasm and give back to life. And then, up comes a dry spot. Burnout. An arid landscape withers the juiciness of life, and things we found tasty are now tinged with burnout's tart and bitter flavors: we become jaded, passive-aggressive, sarcastic, lifeless, nay-saying, contemptuous. Our resignation and resentment dim life's shine.

All of these share a common denominator: unmet expectations. Things haven't worked out the way we think they should. Here's an example from the mideighties, when I was the zen center's resident monk, in my flying-nun phase, robes flurrying, everywhere at once, making sure things happened. Probably some people bought my act; certainly I did. Then someone arrived who took an active dislike to me, and spread rumors, true and false. The theme: I was single-handedly responsible for the decline of Zen in the West. I was thunderstruck; wasn't "I" the one who had done so much, for so many, for so long? Wasn't "I" the busiest little bee at the zen center? I, I, I. Do you hear a little martyrdom?

One morning my cork popped. I'd had it with ringing bells for meditation periods and answering the door in the middle of the night. No more trying so hard and still being disrespected! Obviously, thought echoing hadn't yet taken hold in my practice. Throwing my professed compassion to the winds, I took a break from the daily schedule. Prior to that, I'd never missed a single sitting period. Just then I was stricken with a bout of pneumonia, and I hoped that it would be obvious to everyone how indispensable I was. I felt a shred of relief upon realizing that my absence would be legitimized.

Emergency meetings were held to figure out how to keep the place going, and for a week people came by to see how I was or to learn a procedure. For the next three weeks, the center got along just fine without me. It was like dying and watching things go their merry way without me.

One incident during that month-long stint of pneumonia engendered a small existential crisis concerning control and letting go. I was scheduled to play a harpsichord concert with Anthony Newman, an award-winning humanitarian, musician, and strong spiritual practitioner. Eager to play, I tried everything imaginable to get back my strength. Finally, it was undeniable that I was far too sick to negotiate the athletic repertoire we had planned. I could barely sit up. I notified Tony, and on two days' notice, he pulled Bach's behemoth Goldberg Variations out of his sleeve and gave a brilliant performance.

This episode shook loose my ill-founded belief that I could pull off just about anything I set my mind to, a relic of my longtime control strategy. This failed to take into account the interweaving net of influences. I had to face some facts of life: illness, stress, ambitiousness, exhaustion, burnout.

Which of my many me's could claim to have given me pneumonia? Which was unable to let go of it and play the concert?

Assigning the "I" to the spurious position of deity is a guaranteed prelude to burnout. Letting go clearly wasn't within my power. My best remaininging option was "letting be" or "letting stay"; both are also translations of *upeksha,* as is "equanimity," an invaluable seed of awakening. Equanimity arises as we provide hospitality for whatever guests are currently in our home.

Some unrecognized beliefs that I had brought to zen practice turned out to be harbingers of burnout as well: "If I try harder than everyone else, they'll have to appreciate me"; "If I win at zen, the success will ease my aching heart"; "If I seem to be playing at the top of my game, maybe they won't discover that I don't really know the game." Finally I understood Benjamin Franklin's comment about how despair ruins some, but presumptions many.

I had been sliding toward burnout for quite a while. The buildup can be subtle, since many of the associated beliefs sound like the American dream: doing the right thing will produce positive results, and meaningful activity will alleviate low self-esteem. What happens when we do all the right things and still don't get the results we want? Or get what we want and still feel inadequate?

As hopes fade, people react differently. Some keep going through the motions lifelessly. For others, preburnout can mimic brightly burning aspiration: we might take on increased attachment to rituals or teachers, or go into overdrive with our involvement: "I'm so busy keeping the place going that I don't have time to meditate." We may not notice that we're attempting to outrun sinking feelings that are gaining on us.

Willpower, Won't Power, and Willingness

When burning aspiration declines and burnout sets in, sometimes people express the view that their practice has let them down. M. T. Head says, "You can only be let down if you're leaning on something." What are we trying to lean on—people, a distorted view of what spiritual practice can offer, or a misguided faith in our own willpower? The problem with willpower is that it fails to take into account the potency of "won't power," the resistance that revs up when we realize that our strategies can't dictate reality. As M. T. Head puts it, "When the ego is involved, where there's a will, there's a won't."

In addition to having thoughts of being let down, as burnout mounts, people sometimes conclude that a zen practice is too hard. But where is the hardness really? Could the hardness be in us—hardheaded, hard-nosed, hard-hearted? The assumption that zen practice is too hard might be a blend of won't power, want power (the needy-greedies), bad me, and sour filling.

Willpower, like won't power, is an ego hybrid of willingness, one of the seeds of awakening. Genuine willingness is best encountered by traipsing consciously through the brambles of won't power, which, paradoxically, starts the process of activating willingness.

Until we see what fuels burnout, we're likely to aggravate its symptoms. While we rehash the world's conflagrations, if there's some legitimate issue that could use our assistance, we may find ourselves passively immobilized, griping with people who can't—or won't—take constructive action. And neither do we.

The practical approach for clarifying burnout starts with a conscious decision to refrain from suppressing or indulging burnout's soliloquy.

Thought echoing acts as a mental teleprompter, highlighting the script of impending burnout, that almost-subliminal mental dialogue that runs much like the ticker tape at the bottom of television news programs. Staying grounded in the physical dimension enables the experiencer to function, while open awareness allows the observer to keep an eye on things.

Before burnout descends into chronic cynicism or depression, we need to ask ourselves daily: Is it clear what the point of practice is? What's most important? This doesn't mean sitting around taking our psychic temperature but actively remembering that aspiration requires reminders.

Without the laser eye of practice, our burning aspiration can slowly sink, taking our buoyant spirit with it. If our first thought on hearing this is "What buoyant spirit?" burnout's soot may already be tarnishing our vision. In spite of the discouraging commentary of our grumpiest acquaintances and thoughts, burnout isn't an accurate response to life. Unchecked, it can fry aspiration to a crisp. Diligent, sometimes dogged, practice eventually fertilizes the field where the seeds of perseverance and inspiration are nestled. As enthusiasm is rekindled, enlivenment can emerge phoenixlike from burnout's ashes, transmuting burnout into burning aspiration.

Three Breaths of Awareness: A Meditation

Probably it was in *Readers' Digest* that I first encountered the idea of taking a few deep breaths when you feel stressed. It isn't profound, yet such a simple thing can slow down emotional rush-hour traffic enough to prevent a collision.

meditation's simplicity and specificity is hard to misinterpret, when we're almost overwhelmed. The mind is surprisingly will- to tolerate short bursts of attentiveness. The applications of three reaths are almost unlimited; the ones listed here can be a springboard for coming up with your own versions.

- Whenever stress is strong, feel the sensations and movements of your breathing for three breaths.
- To refresh bodily awareness, take three deeper breaths.
- When feeling irritated or upset, stay with the feeling for three breaths.
- To reground yourself physically, stay conscious of as much of your entire body as possible for three breaths.
- When feeling distracted, attend to what's actually going on, be it painful, wondrous, or uninteresting, for three breaths.
- To remain mindful of neutral activities, intensify your awareness of things you usually find boring for three breaths.
- To be fully aware of pleasurable activities, notice your environs consciously for three breaths.
- When repetitive thoughts plague your airwaves, let your mental tape loops play full-bore for three breaths.
- In almost any situation, pay attention to whatever grabs your attention, and attend to it fully for three breaths.

After one round of the Three Breaths of Awareness meditation, let attention turn to your bodily sensations for three more breaths, before including the environment for three additional breaths. For a final round of breaths, as much as possible, experience everything simultaneously. Sometimes it's appropriate to go for more than one round.

All of these can serve notice on old repetitive thought patterns, telling them that their days of running unabated are numbered. The little mind doesn't always take well to instructions like this, so why not offer the curmudgeonly ego a little treat for doing the exercise? You can encourage your mind to indulge a bit after the exercise, perhaps with a cup of tea. The principle is the same as taking a petulant child (or partner) to the market: when a tantrum looms, we say, "How about going down three more aisles, and then we'll leave through the checkout line with the fruit chews you like?" Far from being cowardly capitulation, this is a harmless way to enroll the "you can't make me" mind in a project that respects its short attention span. Sometimes when we offer the ego free rein for a bit, it may refuse, stamping its foot like a two-year-old: "Not on *your* time frame!" Why not invite your mind to run rampant for a bit and see what happens? When I first tried this, there it was: the very stillness and silence that I'd been struggling to experience.

17 Core Pain

Each difficult moment has the potential to open my eyes and open ✓
my heart.
MYLA KABAT-ZINN

H AVE YOU EVER FELT a heaviness, a sinking sensation, or a
fiery spear that blindsides you as if from nowhere? Have you suddenly shriveled when someone said or did that one thing you thought you
couldn't bear? Up comes a wave of anguish that can't be stifled or outrun.
If this sounds familiar, you're in the neighborhood of core pain. People
who are prone to numbness or denial may believe that they're exempt
from all this; even those of us who suspect it is aboard might hope that it
can be blipped away, by a teacher, tradition, or technique.

Sometimes the resurfacing of long-avoided core pain seems more
intense than actual events seem to warrant—that is, to bystanders. What

makes core pain so powerful is the fact that it has been set aside for so long. We'd do well to view it as a ticking time bomb.

Finally, after we try all the evasions and fixes we can come up with, there comes a point when it's undeniable: core pain is our longtime fellow traveler. Even brushes with the absolute don't eradicate its sting permanently, and when its call becomes urgent, like an appendix on the verge of bursting, we must attend to it. People respond differently when core pain comes surging forth. Some crumble in shame, others wear the pain on their sleeve, seemingly as a tribute to their beloved—the core pain that seems to be the one thing we can count on. Cool customers may seem immune, but look deeper: how often does a romantic's broken heart beat within a cynic's hardened shell?

Core pain is so unacceptable, so socially off-limits, that it is rarely mentioned except in desperate moments. Saint John of the Cross's poetry is atremble with the dark night of the soul, the sting of existential core pain.

Once we acknowledge the presence of core pain, we may not be able to recall a time that it didn't whisper its presence. You can see it in young children, sitting dejected, as if pondering: "It hurts so much when they pick on [or yell at, ridicule, ignore] me. Why do they do it? Oh, I know! It must be because I'm . . . unlovable . . . unworthy . . . not good enough." Do you see what just happened? The youngster, in trying to make sense of the pain, actually compounds it by grafting on a presumed reason—usually in the form of a negative self-identity. The process doubles the pain; now we not only feel bad, we believe we *are* bad, fundamentally flawed in some way. Small children can't bear this much pain, so it sinks from view like ruins in the Yucatan, covered by a jungle of protections and evasions. In the process, the bright wonder-full-ness we admire in tiny faces dims. And then we grow up, our secret buried under the thicket of socialization.

Over time, it becomes harder to maintain our cover-ups. Even if we sense that something needs attending, we may fear that if we go there, we'll never recover. So evasion increases our insulation, making core pain even more off-limits. At last, it starts to surface, and the grenades that have lain buried in the jungle are now lobbed into our lives.

Engaging Core Pain Experientially

There comes a point at which we have no choice but to engage core pain in a conscious, healing way. Then we're fortunate to be grounded in meditations that feature the chest center as a primary checkpoint—sensory solace for the yearning ache that might be welling up in midtorso.

Sometimes core pain emerges when there isn't time for addressing it on the spot. When that happens, it's almost always possible to put the pain on hold for a time and return later, via meditations in the emotional dimension section. We're quite familiar with putting core pain on hold; we've been doing it unconsciously for years. Now, consciously, we can relate to it the same way we relate to the need to attend to several tasks simultaneously. However, we must return later, allowing core pain to metabolize experientially, or it will reenter the well of unhealed suffering.

Sometimes meditators assume that if something isn't happening in the moment, it doesn't need to be dealt with. This kind of thinking underestimates the power of the conditioned parrot, which is deeply ensconced and may not pipe up constantly.

Until we realize that core pain lurks in our own depths, we will probably keep our hypervigilant gaze turned outward, fearing an attack from out there somewhere. Little do we realize that core pain can't be kept out, since it's already in. Thus it lurks, surfacing periodically like a shark, taking bites out of our aliveness.

Healing is best served by addressing all five dimensions of awakening—physical, mental, emotional, open awareness, and full-empty—since core pain encompasses them all. What do we find when we open the vault? A misery deposit, consisting of the painful physical, mental, and emotional components that have been festering during years of neglect.

As the breath pervades core pain, we sense that it isn't an intolerable solitary cell. As environmental awareness joins in, it provides a holding space. What more could our core pain wish for than to be met with the merciful kindness we would extend to a frightened animal or another person in similar circumstances? Can't you hear the silent whisper, "Please, how about some tenderness here?"

Given the extent to which we have abandoned our pain, we must now adopt it. In relation to core pain, spiritual practice isn't a bypass operation—it's of the open-heart persuasion. If we start to wonder where the joy is in all of this, how about considering the words of the philosopher and zen afficionado Alan Watts, who said often that without being more sensitive to pain, we can't be sensitive to pleasure either.

When the ship of life collides with the submerged iceberg of core pain, we have an opportunity to visit the seeds of patience, perseverance, and willingness. One of the greatest gifts of the path of awakening is the discovery that, to our amazement, embracing core pain compassionately opens the door of heartmind.

Adversity and Awakening: A Meditation on Healing Deep Suffering

The Adversity and Awakening meditation provides an alternative to unworkable approaches like attempting to drop the pain or shut it out, or to the contrary, falling headlong into it.

We invite in something that we find distressing, something that brings up such seemingly intractable tribulations as loss, grief, or discouragement.

Until the process becomes familiar, it helps to keep the following instructions beside you when you do the meditation.

- *Position.* Begin with your back erect and your chest as open as possible. Feel the sensations throughout your body, elevating the head and upper torso naturally with the breath.
- *Issue.* Let the disheartening situation come to mind.
- *Physical feelings.* Feel your least-wanted bodily sensation, for a few breaths' time.
- *Heart or grief point.* Now bring attention to the center of the chest. Several fingertips of one hand can rest on the tender spot midsternum, which will be the touchpoint, even if your strongest sensations are elsewhere. The chest center functions as a conduit through which everything—air, the residual sensations, anything at all—can be experienced physically on subsequent inhalations. On the exhalations, let things be rather than attempt to do anything.

- *Most anguishing belief.* See if there is some strong belief about yourself, a situation, or life in general, while also maintaining awareness of the center of your chest.
- *Decline internal monologue.* After listening respectfully to the strong belief you just encountered, decline the monologue's offer to continue. Unless the focus remains physical, core pain will be reinforced.
- *Uncomfortable sensations.* Again, feel any unwanted sensations, on an inhalation.
- *Letting be on the exhalation.* After inhaling whatever sensations are present, on the exhalation and then for a few subsequent breaths let everything be. Repeat this step several times, alternating between breathing in painful sensations and residue on the inhalation and letting be on the exhalation.
- *Breath.* For a few full breaths, feel how the bodily feelings are ventilated by the breath. Reinvite any unwanted sensations to be included.
- *Breath stream.* Now bring awareness to the breath stream, a conduit connecting the air of breathing and the air of the room or area.
- *Finish.* Let attention encompass the body, sounds, air texture, and shapes that are present. Rest in the totality of air-pain-breath-room-sky for as long as you like.

Your posture may have collapsed somewhat, since core pain and discouragement tend to pull us into a caved-in position. Feel the collapsed sensations briefly, and then let the breath invite your body to expand, lengthening on the inhalations and softening on the exhalations, supported by the waves of the breath.

The process is bound to be somewhat uncomfortable, just as surgery may initially make things seem worse than the illness it is intended to address. This process is about seeing and doing things in a new way, and even the feelings of openness and balance might seem slightly unnerving if we're not too familiar with them.

One of the most challenging parts of the process is learning to distinguish between letting things be and attempting to let go, to make the unwanted go away by being dropped. This is a veiled attempt to get rid of what we want nothing to do with, and if it worked, we'd be awake and free by now. In contrast to what we hoped, this makes the pain seem intractable. We have to hear this hundreds of times, since it's counterintuitive. By contrast, the gentle inclusiveness of letting be provides a tender welcome to what has long been rejected. It's a little like putting a chili pepper in a stew rather than trying to eat it straight. The pepper is still there, but it no longer seems like the only thing.

This meditation is an enterprise of inclusion rather than exclusion. Never underestimate the power of ceasing to resist what's at hand. As we enter the moment fully, we find that painful feelings are as porous and insubstantial as everything else.

This meditation is an opportunity to be "healed in our suffering," as one of the verses we say regularly at ZCSD puts it. As our knots of suffering are saturated by space and throb with our heartbeat, the inclusivity that we experience is a reminder that we're never alone, that equanimity and compassion lie in an entirely different direction than we have suspected.

Hitting Bottom: Opening into the Ocean of Grief, Loss, and Despair

How do you pick up a rock at the bottom of Ise Bay without getting wet?
ZEN KOAN

Sometimes life seems to flow smoothly, at least in our little corner of things. If that's the case in the early phases of our spiritual practice, we may take inspiration from zen phrases like "no loss and no gain," words that pay tribute to the empty aspect of full-emptiness, zen's absolute. If we have a philosophical bent or a fondness for transcendent, empty-absolute perspectives, we may not yet realize that the absolute shows up garbed in the relative forms that constitute the full side of full-emptiness. If our perspective has been one-sided, emphasizing only emptiness, when we hear someone mention hitting bottom we may invoke rhetoric to the effect that there is no bottom and no one to hit bottom.

And then we hit bottom. It could be the death of a loved one, a grave physical diagnosis, having done something we consider unforgiveable, a nightmarish relationship change, or the reemergence of a destructive habit that we believed was behind us. Do you have an example?

We're suddenly tumbled from the shallow waters into a whirlpool that pulls us to the bottom of Ise Bay. This koan alludes to a bay in Japan and is sometimes considered to be one of a handful of classic zen koans that provide a whiff of emotion. With or without the koan reference, the analogy of facing the bottom of a bay evokes the unfathomable depths, including the reservoir of sorrow and grief that are among the most afflictive emotions.

When I first came to zen, my response to moderately painful things was to maintain a cheery can-do functionality. Even if I felt crushed, my veiled internal stance amounted to, "I won't give them the satisfaction of seeing how hurt I am." I was simultaneously finding solace and refreshment through opening into some zen koans that were profoundly moving and realizing that on another level I was seeking a kind of refuge in my immature and limited sense of the nature of emptiness.

Then a seemingly innocuous event tumbled me into a well of agony. I now understood without any doubt that formal practice must be applicable in devastating upwellings like this one. How else could we recognize the hardest times as forms of emptiness?

Before the bottom falls out, we may not know that we are sitting on a landfill of unmined grief. When the bottom falls out, we see the limitation of phrases like "time heals," since we're facing something that we thought time had already healed. Things we thought we could count on are shattered. It isn't pretty, as we moan or crawl in agony, our throbbing lacerations becoming raw and ragged.

If our worldview collapses sufficiently, it may temporarily eclipse our wish to awaken. Our suffering adheres to an isolated self that is shorn of its customary ego veneer. Now we understand Christ's words on the cross, which boil down to "Take this away from me."

The ego is pretty useless when we hit bottom; in fact, it's the ego that hits bottom. This, however, is a koan to be lived experientially.

If the pain subsides a bit, we may delude ourselves that Humpty Dumpty is back together again. On goes our facade, and we head to the medicine chest of comforting activities, substances, and subterfuges. We may try to avoid hitting bottom by hitting out: we may want the others who are implicated in our situation to hurt as much as we do. We use

:ds or actions as scabs of resentment, hoping to conceal our despera-
1 and dull the pain.

Finally, avoidance is futile. The pain is within our perimeter and must
be addressed there. Unexamined, the toxicity is like blood poisoning, un-
dermining our life force. If things get to the point that grief and anguish are
shaking us apart or our thoughts and moods are so bleak that we question
the point of living, it's time to reach out for help. Unattended, the voices of
devastation can lead us into dangerous territory. We shouldn't be too
proud; in fact, pride and stoicism are regarded as blinders in most spiritual
traditions. A plethora of skillful therapeutic modalities complement formal practice at such times. This is a time to speak with a teacher or practice
consultant who is experienced in working with adversity as part of the path
of awakening. If our mind tells us we're beyond help, hopefully we have a
wise friend who will remind us, kindly, that this is the trained parrot at its
worst. In general, it's better not to talk to too many people, particularly
those who are prone to sympathetic justifications or pity, since their input
can feed our self-pity or the belief that we're helpless. We're fortunate indeed if someone close to us has the capacity to simply be present and listen.

As allies, certain standby practice-awareness tools that we have already
encountered can be managed even when we're hitting bottom. In addition
to the upcoming One Breath meditation, some of the key supports at such
a time include

- knowing our strongly believed thoughts;
- remembering *and,* the one-word reminder that invites awareness into
  areas that may be lost to view, in the physical *and* mental *and* emotional dimensions, *and* the open awareness dimension, which allows
  the residual pain of hitting bottom to merge with global awareness;

- pausing to take three breaths, a practice pause for a short and explicit duration;
- saying "not now" to our thoughts (this is rarely recommended but may be necessary if anguished thoughts feed our despair);
- bringing awareness to the chest center: more than ever, this checkpoint is invaluable now. It is considered a pièce de résistance for awakening within the deepest grief. Interestingly, traditional Chinese medicine considers that grief and joy unite in this central dwelling space.

All of these practices are portable, capable of being carried, and of carrying us, through a lifetime. In times of duress, we will have to engage them intentionally, perhaps needing the support of others as a reminder. This is one of the most powerful functions of the group presence in formal meditation settings, given that awareness of just about everything flees when the abyss opens.

The Shell, the Pain, and the Heart: What Breaks?

Haven't we all known the pain of having someone turn away when we're hurting? Yet we regularly turn away from our own pain, thus intensifying it. At times of fierce emotional pain, I used to believe that shards of anguish were stabbing my heart, and called this heartbreak or heartache. While we might refer to this as relating to the "small heart" of ego, perhaps a more faithful description is that the protective shell we've tried to erect around our tender heart is what is pierced, allowing long-accumulated pain to pour forth. Now there's a possibility of attending to unfinished business that has been stowed away.

See if you can feel, and perhaps envision, the way these different aspects relate: the protective shell or cocoon; the pain; and the unfathomable heart of vastness, which is spacious enough to contain whatever is calling out for inclusion. As the shell breaks open and the pain is embraced, we see that the heart of vastness can't be broken. Nor does it need to open; it is always open.

A valuable practice koan is: what keeps us from directly encountering the always-available heart of vastness? There may come a time that we appreciate hitting bottom, as a turning point toward wakefulness. But probably not until we've gone through what seems like a death of sorts. Pushed to the wall with no wiggle room, we finally take up our burden and may be surprised to find it lighter when taken up than when we reject it.

Descending to the depths, supported by a comprehensive practice, we may find, as if through grace, that compassion abides at the roots of grief. Now we see that the me-self, which is only a speck, a mote in the eye of being-awareness, is a speck that can blind us. Now the following words by Rashani resound:

> There is a hollow space
> too vast for words
> through which we pass
> with each loss,
> out of whose darkness
> we are sanctioned into being.
> —RASHANI RÉA, SELF-PUBLISHED

ᐯ May the contemplation of hitting bottom renew our aspiration and resolve to enter the depths and attest to the reality of heartmind.

One Breath of Healing: A Meditation of Including and Extending

> True love and prayer are learned in the hour when love becomes impossible and the heart has turned to stone.

THOMAS MERTON

When seemingly disabling circumstances arise, sometimes all we can muster is utter simplicity. One breath at a time.

The One Breath of Healing meditation heals in the sense of returning us to our innate wholeness, breath by breath. We include whatever discord is present on an inhale and experience it as fully as possible. On a succeeding exhale, we can simply let it be or attempt the more active approach below.

The One Breath of Healing meditation starts by bringing our attention to the breath. We let our pained mind know that its heaviest thoughts can either have a rest for a few moments or be included with the breath, provided they don't try to prevail. Then:

Including. On an inhale, breathe in your overall sense of suffering as fully as possible, almost like a reverse sigh. This can be global or centered in the chest. Taking slightly deeper breaths at first may be helpful.

Extending. On an exhale, let your awareness and breath suffuse your entire being as much as possible.

If it seems appropriate, you can include a phrase or mantra on each exhale, or even on each inhale too in dire moments. I've found the following words helpful in maintaining some sense of presence and motivation: "May compassion awaken," or "wholeness," or "mercy," or "oneness." There have, however, been other times when a nonverbal cry was all that was possible. Corinthians 12:9, "In my weakness is my strength," is a koan that the One Breath meditation may resolve.

If an aspiration arises to have healing (health and wholeness) permeate our suffering, that too can be extended, via an exhale, throughout our body or in whatever direction speaks to us.

The nature of despair is such that it's easy to lose sight of our connectedness at such times, and we fall into a sequestered feeling of aloneness. The One Breath of Healing meditation may provide a bridge back to openness.

Additional repetitions of the One Breath of Healing meditation are fine: one breath, then another, and another. When words aren't possible, it's sufficient to feel the breath.

The One Breath of Healing meditation can be, in a sense, a vow: a visceral reminder of our wish to awaken from the dream of self, which is at the root of so much affliction. This wish is echoed in formal zen services: "May compassion be extended to all beings." In grave times when a cure for our ills seems unlikely, we wish for the healing awareness of encountering our completeness.

In my many years of practice, there have been times when the One Breath of Healing practice has been my main return route for remembering that "my suffering" is also *the* suffering—the universal suffering of all beings. This is a conduit into empathy and interconnectedness, perhaps starting with people in similar circumstances and then extending into the compass of all beings.

The similarity between the One Breath of Healing meditation and the first two lines of the Loving-Kindness meditation makes Loving-Kindness a worthwhile next step as things begin to settle somewhat, a gravitational pull to awaken the seeds of heartmind.

18 Reconciliation, Atonement, Forgiveness

THE TEMPLE GUARDIANS AT THE GATES OF THE FULL-EMPTY DIMENSION

For all the harm I have caused others, intentionally or unintentionally, I ask forgiveness. For all the harm that I have caused myself, intentionally or unintentionally, I forgive myself. For all the harm that others have caused me, intentionally or unintentionally, I forgive them.

WORDS OF ATONEMENT, ZEN CENTER OF LOS ANGELES

So FAR, WE HAVE been meeting full-emptiness indirectly, through empirical exercises. Our indirect approach is similar to the way you meet a young child or a cat. Rather than going right up to them, you hang out in their vicinity and attend to something else, sniffing flowers or listening to passing traffic. Eventually they come over and check you out.

Full-emptiness is like that; to try to head for it directly, or to speak too much of it prematurely, is like holding up your hand in front of someone and saying, "Isn't this amazing? It's a hand!" You'd get some raised eyebrows at the implication that something so direct should be called attention to as if it were extraordinary. A hand is such a natural thing, and so is full-emptiness, whether we realize it or not. As we investigate the other dimensions, full-empty awareness sneaks up, like the cat or child. It creeps up stealthily on cat's feet, tempted by the sprouting catnip of heartmind.

For compassion and wisdom to thrive, we must bring special consideration to the pernicious seeds that have already sent forth shoots—the ego hybrids of resentment, blame, shame, and jealousy. These can seem intractable until they are warmed in the light of reconciliation, atonement, and forgiveness, along with the precepts, or guidelines, for living-as-if-awake.

Through mindful investigation, open awareness, and loving-kindness, we can start to appreciate the whole meal, which we've only sampled so far. As we come into the home stretch, we can revisit this koan: "What, in this moment, could actually block the fullness of the moment?" Questions like that, which require experiential contemplation, can help entice our inherent wisdom forth, to reveal the ever-present full-emptiness and compassion at the core of our being.

Of all the terrain we traverse in a lifetime of zen practice, reconciliation is among the harshest. It has two aspects: atonement, where we see ourselves as having fallen short, and forgiveness, where we blame another. These twin gateposts qualify as contenders for temple guardians at the gate of our true home.

Until we greet and befriend these guards, the gateless gate may seem blocked by the ghosts of past events, including the ones that never happened, like grudges based on a misunderstanding. Let's see if entering these desolate climes can help reveal a fundamental truth of practice: that there has never been any barrier to the realm of full-emptiness.

Atonement: At-one-ment

Never give up on yourself; then you'll never give up on anyone else either.

PEMA CHÖDRÖN

When my former husband was a teenager, a twelve-year-old boy ran in front of his car and was killed instantly. It was completely unavoidable, yet it has replayed hauntingly over his life. Probably we've all had memory flashes in which we recall something we would never have done if we had been ourselves. Waves of shame or guilt leave us wondering if we'll ever know forgiveness; we hardly realize that we ourselves are the most unforgiving of all.

No one is faultless or impeccable here. We all have something calling for atonement. Most spiritual paths have observances that acknowledge the felt need for repentance or atonement: Ramadan, Yom Kippur, confession, Lent, Twelve-step amends, and Buddhist full moon ceremonies. In zen, major life transitions, like weddings, include an atonement ceremony in which the words extend beyond the personal into life at large, saying "all suffering" rather than just "suffering caused by me," as a reminder of our essential connectedness. In truth, most of the harm we do results from seeing ourselves as isolated entities, so a prime task of spiritual inquiry is to investigate how we keep divisiveness in its ill-gotten seat, claiming false dominion over our lives.

Oneness doesn't mean we can afford to overlook the specific harm we've caused, so we have to start with what's on our own plate. The things calling for atonement may range from a crime to a seemingly innocuous action, like ignoring the hello of a homeless person we suspect wants something from us.

If we're used to beating up on ourselves, we might confuse atonement with self-flagellation, we might see ourselves as basically nice and question whether we have anything to atone for. In either case, we might want to consider this quote from Stephen Levine to see if anything jumps out: "I ask your forgiveness for however I may have caused you pain in the past through my anger, my lust, my fear, my ignorance, my blindness, my doubt, my confusion. However I may have caused you pain, I ask that you let me back into your heart."* This short, powerful compendium of ways we cause distress to others echoes the Episcopal Book of Common Prayer's reference to things done and things left undone.

If our tendency has been to dwell on the cruelty of others—possibly with whole narratives memorized—we now recognize that we too have been victimizers. Our blaming tendencies have come home to roost.

Seeing the magnitude of what we have been up to can cause an up-welling of guilt and shame, yet this is not the direction of healing. Guilt and shame only drive the stake of pain deeper. When we see how much guilt we carry, we understand how guilt can become institutionalized in

* Stephen Levine, *Healing into Life and Death* (New York: Anchor Doubleday, 1989).

some families and religions; still, no devil could hold a candle to the way we punish ourselves and others.

ACTIVELY ENGAGING IN ATONEMENT PRACTICE

When we enter the fields of atonement, our primary venture is to reconcile with life directly, not attempt to accrue personal merit, clean the slate, eradicate guilt, or balance accounts through penance. Remorse and conscience press us toward reconciliation, and we may decide to include atonement in our meditation. We want to make amends but may not know how to go about it; a person's whereabouts may be unknown. It may be inappropriate to open another person's old wounds. Or the person in question may no longer be living. What to do?

Having a variety of ways to approach atonement helps to bring life to ritual and thaws feelings that we may have kept frozen. This is an apt time to return to the five dimensions of heartmind. Sit quietly, close your eyes, remember some sorrowful situation, and notice what the five dimensions can tell you:

Physical dimension. Feel the kinesthetic remnants of years of maneuverings and tightening, particularly when guilt takes over.

Open awareness dimension. Include awareness of the environmental ambience to provide a blanket of present reality to warm sad memories.

Mental dimension. Notice any recurring thoughts that are particularly humiliating or shameful.

Emotional dimension. Notice what mind states and moods undergird your remorse and sense of dismay.

Full-empty dimension. How can you challenge your ingrained, limiting notions of selfhood, the roots that underpin the injurious attitudes and actions that sprouted all this grief? A great remedy is the potential to realize, firsthand, that when we hurt another, it is tantamount to cutting off our own arm. If these words sounds grandiose, their message is a counterbalance to our tenacious viewpoints to the contrary.

In addition to applied awareness, reconciliation ceremonies are often a part of formal practice, including vows and precepts, like the guideposts for living-as-if-awake presented in the next chapter. Zen teacher and author Diane Rizzetto wrote an especially applicable aspiration that is generally related to refraining from stealing: "I take up the way of taking only what is freely given and giving freely of all that I can."* Her wording encourages us to reflect broadly on where we feel free to demand things that aren't being offered and also to consider the ways we hold back on giving, perhaps out of a mentality of scarcity.

I try new wording periodically, like this combination of wording from zen, the Twelve Steps (number ten), and one of my favorite reminders, "things done and left undone," from the Book of Common Prayer:† "I acknowledge, atone for, and intend to reconcile the suffering caused by my unskillful thoughts, words, and actions. Furthermore, I vow to receive input willingly, to inventory potential blind spots, and to make amends promptly for things I have done, and left undone." These lines usually jog my memory for specific areas that might otherwise pass unnoticed.

Another tool is an atonement circle. Participants bring up whatever they feel is seeking their attention and resolution, along with possible steps to take, so that their spiritual practice can be brought to bear. Other mem-

---

* Diane Rizzetto, *Waking Up to What We Do* (Boston: Shambhala Publications, 2005).
† The Episcopal Book of Common Prayer (New York: Church Hymnal Corporation, 1979).

bers of the group listen silently, offering the gift of their presence. Confidentiality requires that whatever comes up remains within the confines of the circle. Chatting later on the patio about what occurred in the circle undermines the efficacy of atonement circles.

Sometimes people fear exposure or being seen as unworthy in others' eyes. Really, though, don't you find yourself kindly disposed toward people who honestly own up to what they have done and express the wish for reconciliation and forgiveness? It's so much less painful than isolating ourselves, cutting off relationships, or justifying ourselves.

Another means of atonement is healing action and reconciliation. This involves engaging in activities that profess our wish to live beneficially. Such actions can relate to a specific situation, offering sincere contrition, whether the other accepts it or not. There can also be a symbolic memorial or offering, a way of expressing our regrets and our resolve to begin anew.

One thing that will require regular revisiting is the sobering area of correspondence between our self-contempt and the harm we have done to others. Few candidates for leading us into harmfulness are stronger than the negativity we hold for ourselves. Given the contagion of our self-inflicted disdain, we must take strong measures to put to rest the cycle of self-loathing and the resulting harmful actions.

The quality of mercy is essential for atonement to become a living force. The process must be ongoing, thoroughgoing, and compassionate. Atonement must seep into our molecules, where the old patternings are engraved. This requires that we swallow whole some of the least palatable things on our plate, the heart-wrenching issues that led Thich Nhat Hanh to express the wish that the doors of our hearts be left open.

Atonement takes patience; it takes everything we've got, for as long as we've got. That's a small price to pay, considering the cost of unrepentant unkindness or utter despair. Who can say what it takes for the parched, hardened barricade around our heart to soften? Usually lots of watering, often with tears. Seeing the pain that has resulted from our own missteps opens us to compassion for others—our greater body. When reconciliation finally calls us to turn from what others have done to what we ourselves have done, it increases the likelihood that we will stumble into the realization that the very persons we have seen as them, are us.

Forgiveness

Forgiveness is the fragrance that the violet sheds on the heel that has crushed it.

MARK TWAIN

Sometimes in zen contexts we hear phrases to the effect that we can't harm or be harmed by another. Yet in conventional terms, we can do harmful things and engage in untrustworthy actions.

What does practice entail when we've been on the receiving end of attitudes and actions that range from insensitive to unkind to violent? What serves us in remembering our aspiration to live in accord with the compassion and interconnectedness of our actual nature, or what we might call love? If this issue weren't among the hardest of all things we face in a lifetime, the world would look very different. Forgiveness reverses the atonement scenario; here we believe someone else has caused harm, often to us or to someone close to us. We may cling to begrudging attitudes in the wake of a life-impacting upheaval or a difficult or altered relationship.

Unforgivingness can show up in situations that range from thoughtlessness to conflicting desires to felonies. We're not talking about Hitler here; the situations usually involve people we know or have known, where some action or dynamic has cut to the quick. We temporarily abandon any wish for reunion and recite our litany of grievances, as a protective amulet to ward off further anguish. We never want to feel this way again. They could have done better, and they didn't. They should never have done what they did, but they did. We fear that forgiving them will let them off the hook, excuse their behavior, and perhaps even authorize a recurrence.

We may contemplate revenge; we want the other person to hurt as badly as we do. If the cycle continues unabated for long, we'll have intimate knowledge of the seedbed from which war and family violence sprout.

Before we continue, let's be clear that forgiveness is not portraying ourselves as irreproachable. Forgiveness is not about putting ourselves in situations that practically guarantee a repeat of destructive behavior. Reestablishing personal closeness is best postponed until the forgiveness process is well under way. Sometimes agreements, even legally binding ones, need to be in place, particulary if discord or violence is possible. This isn't meant to sound legalistic but to maintain the most harmonious relationships possible.

Actively Practicing Forgiveness: An Exercise

If our anger is strong, we may have to sneak up sideways on forgiveness, detouring around the emotional dimension. Treading lightly beats rushing. When we contemplate the prospect of disarming ourselves, we may fear becoming defenseless: What if we let our guard down and have no alarm system to warn us? Will we again be cast aside, crumbling in misery? At the very least we'll probably keep our radar intact and rearm our ineffectual security system by taking false comfort in the roles of judge and jury.

Although we may believe that we can't take any more pain, our isolation actually deepens our misery. This is where meditations that address agitation can be useful.

At this juncture, we may need to admit that we're not ready for forgiveness. Owning up to this is better than falling into a pretense of being forgiving, which strengthens our barricade against genuine forgiveness.

Here's one way of doing a status check on whether actively undertaking the forgiveness process is possible at this time. Take a pause, sit quietly, and bring the person involved to mind. Feel whatever bodily sensations arise when you think of this person; then, after feeling this for a few breaths, let your body respond to the question: "Is forgiveness possible at this time?" If there's a jolt or a strong negative response, see whether you can identify a strong thought playing in your mind. If nothing appears, ask, "What would I most like to say to this person?" If something jumps out, that's the thought that needs echoing; hear it respectfully, without adding additional thoughts, so as not to become mired in unforgivingness. Then spend a few more moments feeling whatever is rumbling around on a visceral level, and finish by resting in open awareness for a little, knowing that for now, forgiveness will have to wait.

From the Shallows to the Depths of Forgiveness, and Back

After we've been mired in unwillingness for a while, there may come a point when it's unpalatable to hold on to hurt and resentment. Even if our pain has become colored by martyrdom, we may start to get messages from the underground, reports that we are sitting on a burial mound of sadness and loss. When our heavy heart will no longer be denied, we may feel quietly propelled to move in the direction of forgivingness.

Proceed gently. Again, bring the person involved to mind. Let awareness touch on your sensations, and lend a respectful ear to any quiet thoughts. Spend a brief time here, staying a few breaths longer than is comfortable. As before, finish by resting in open awareness.

As increased willingness to forgive comes, bring your attention to the center of your chest, that spacious chalice; feeling your breathing there, and picture or sense the person on an inhalation. Then on several subsequent breaths, stay for a while, resolved not to be captured by the remnants of hurt you may be tempted to hold on to.

As the forgiveness process deepens, with its alternations of openness and resistance, one of the most restorative courses to take is to continue with your own atonement practice. Few things are more helpful in mitigating the blaming mind and increasing tolerance than finding the very qualities that we condemned in another looking back at us from the mirror. Admitting our own shortcomings and acknowledging our unforgiving streak helps us comprehend something that's hard to see when we're hurting: that just as our own unskillful habits are born of tormenting conditioning, others are in the same boat—including that person we have been so loathe to forgive.

At this point, we might consider saying words like the following in the context of meditative awareness: "Just as my unkindness and harmful actions come from a place of pain and closed-heartedness, I recognize that the same may be true for you. I aspire to reconcile my own attitudes and actions and to live guided by compassion." After saying this, sit quietly for a few more breaths. This may brighten the flame of empathy or, conversely, precipitate an upsurge of resentment that tests our resolve.

When we look honestly at the snail's pace of our own transformation, how can we expect others to move faster than we do? Exiling someone from our life leaves us in exile as well.

Even when we do turn more decisively toward forgiveness, we shouldn't expect to become paragons of benevolence overnight. We may suddenly notice perversely noble thoughts like: "I forgive you, no matter how rotten you are, because I'm kinder than you are." That's not forgiveness; that's self-indulgence.

The path of forgiveness resembles the salmon's upstream swim in the interest of renewed life. There will be whitewater and rapids, sometimes turbulence that tempts us to go back down the old paths. The trail of forgiveness is long and twisted.

We may undergo many travails before we appreciate Mark Twain's reflection that we are not only the crushed violet and the fragrance left on the crushing heel but the heel as well, at times. This heart-wrenching realization intensifies our comprehension that without pain, compassion is unlikely.

19 *Living As One*

All that is necessary for negativity to triumph is for good people to say and do nothing when harmful things transpire.
MAHATMA GANDHI

I N   M Y   E A R L Y   Y E A R S   of practice, aglow from some opening experiences and immersion in koan study, I took a sabbatical from university teaching to live at a zen center. The first night, turning on the light in my room in the recently purchased old building, I found the place blanketed with thousands of roaches. I ran out and slept in the meditation hall. The next day, wondering how to proceed, I looked to one of zen's precepts: "Do not kill." Hmmm, does that apply to roaches? Then I found a koan commentary about dying with what dies, and that sounded like my brand of nonduality; obviously the enlightened thing would be to die with them, koan style, killing them with my bare hands, while chanting the Heart Sutra, which was one of the main scriptures (sutras) recited at that zen center. That night I mashed them open-handedly in the dark, trying to kill them instantly so they wouldn't suffer. My chanting barely masked the sound of their tiny bodies being squished. The third day I'd had it, and I bought a roach bomb.

What actually died, along with my thousands of little roommates, was my presumption of being somewhat awake. Tellingly, it never occurred to me to include the roaches in the atonement ceremony that was part of my regular practice. Until then my view of zen had been unbalanced in favor of the absolute, or emptiness, a symptom of delusion in light of the inextricable interweaving of the absolute and relative dimensions as they relate to walking, talking, and living.

This situation was a fairly mild example, though not to the roaches, of misinterpreting spiritual practice to serve egocentric perspectives. This is the opposite of compassion; the tilt is toward narcissism, or possibly a sociopathic mentality, as a justification for those in whom conscience and kindness are dormant.

Malpractice

With all our references to practice, is there such a thing as malpractice? Definitely. Malpractice distorts spiritual principles to the ego's ends, or replaces our individual ego with a spiritual one. Then there's "true believerism": the hope to be told what to think and do, in hopes of fitting in or being cared for. This pursuit escalates malpractice from a misdemeanor to a felony if participants look the other way when they see something going on that would get a corporate CEO arrested. If there's a presumption in a spiritual group that leaders or participants have transcended ordinarily sanctioned standards of behavior, or if dubious actions are presented as teaching that we don't yet understand, or even crazy wisdom, what is being served? If such justifications cross our minds (or lips), discernment needs some refurbishing. We can't afford to leave our common sense on the shoe rack with our sandals.

One of the most important steps toward spiritual maturity is learning when it's time to vote with our feet. Spiritual groups have a mandate to provide a beneficial environment, with the leadership setting the example. The first zen precept mirrors the Hippocratic oath in proclaiming: At least do no harm. When my mother heard about the shenanigans in one group, she said, "How can this be happening? Aren't zen people supposed to be interested in waking up? This sounds as asleep as the man in the street."

Zen speaks of the need for realization, or awakening to reality, in baby steps, giant steps, and no steps at all. Yet even more significant is actualization, living in accord with whatever realizations may come along. Beneficial living can't wait; sometimes we're more awake than at other times. But what about when we're not so awake? Decades into spiritual practice, old blind spots can reemerge, and a prescription adjustment will be required for clear seeing to be possible.

In addition to the supports that have already been mentioned, if you're bold, you might consider getting some input from your mate, your mom, or your manager. Their assessments may not classify as great wisdom, but they might clarify whether or not our presumed spiritual insights are making the trip from our meditation seat to daily life. Besides, listening to their opinions is a great test of humility!

For further guidance, we can turn to zen's precepts.

Precepts: Guideposts for Living-As-If-Awake

If you don't live it, it won't come out your horn.

CHARLIE PARKER

Penetrating to the marrow of zen's precepts is considered such a formidable undertaking that they are considered in depth after the completion of koan study. The precepts reflect the natural functioning that ensues when we see all existence as our very body. However, since such times are likely to be intermittent, it's a boon to have mirrors that reflect areas where our vision is obstructed.

We don't need to be fully awake to live-as-if-awake; that's where the precepts come in. We may not have much trouble understanding the ramifications of gross actions like killing and stealing; it's the subtle things, like keeping agreements and being trustworthy, that sneak up on us.

The precepts encourage us to live in ways that are beneficial to all. The problem is that after years of self-centered perception and action, we may not be inclined to give up our self-serving ways, even if we know they make us miserable.

So how do precepts move from good ideas to a lived reality? We can start by thinking of places in our life and our practice that are particularly cloudy, at least on occasion, and select one precept that speaks to us situationally or in general. Then we can observe subtle and gross misalignments in our daily interactions, in conjunction with applied practice, or WIPITS (what is practice in this situation?), since just having guidelines isn't enough. They need to be backed up with some how-to.

It would take an entire book to do justice to the precepts, and excellent ones are available. The challenges abound; it's tempting to word the precepts as injunctions, but as Marshall Rosenberg, founder of the Center for Nonviolent Communication and a longtime mentor to me, has said, it's pretty hard to do a don't.

The first line of each precept is "I vow," which sounds more accountable than "I plan to," "I hope to," or "I'll try." "I'll try" often means "Oh, well . . . maybe," giving ourselves a big out. We don't want to set ourselves up with outs before we're even in. We don't want to take up a punitive stance either, as the point is encouragement, not just to be awake in our actions, but to contact our inherent inter-being, which means living in alignment with the precepts. The precepts are interpreted on all sorts of levels; yet if our functioning is out of alignment with on-the-street notions of appropriate and compassionate functioning, we might want to look a little more closely at what we're up to.

Perhaps the best way to regard these precepts, as stated here, is as aspirations assisting us in remembering what's most important. Each precept's description is followed by more traditional wording in parentheses.

The Three Primary Precepts, or Aspirations

These three precepts remind us of the interconnectedness of everything and encourage us to take to heart the following qualities:

1. Non-harmfulness. I vow to abstain from indulging in harmful thoughts, words, and actions. (Like the Hippocratic oath, refrain from causing harm.)

2. Benefaction. I vow to act beneficially, on behalf of all concerned. (Be life centered, do good.)

3. Inclusivity. I vow to awaken to the inherent nature of existence and consciously manifest and serve our inherent unity. (Serve all life.)

THE TEN APPLIED PRECEPTS, OR ASPIRATIONS

The following ten applied zen precepts remind us to bring heartmind to bear in all that we say and do:

1. Cherish life. I vow to serve existence from a life-centered perspective (refraining from killing and cruelty).

2. Receive and give. I vow to take and give only what is freely offered, or can be given or received, appropriately and openly (refraining from stealing).

3. Respect intimacy. I vow to engage in appropriate physical and relational intimacy (refraining from misusing sexuality).

4. Speak compassionately. I vow to speak that which is factually accurate, kindly intentioned, beneficial to all involved, necessary, and timely (refraining from lying).

5. Maintain unclouded mental functioning. I vow to base my words and actions on clear thinking and seeing (refraining from intoxicating substances).

6. Emphasize the constructive. I vow to discover the best in people (refraining from speaking of the faults of others).

7. Acknowledge equality. I vow to function in accord with the equality and unity of all (refraining from elevating the self and putting down others).

8. Practice generosity. I vow to give generously and appropriately of my time, energy, and resources (refraining from withholding assets unnecessarily).

9. Manifest equanimity. I vow to act and speak harmoniously when difficult situations arise (refraining from indulging anger and other disconnecting emotions).

10. Respect unity. I vow to honor the aspiration that underlies diverse spiritual traditions (refraining from speaking ill of teachings, in whatever form they appear).

Communication and Listening

I spent a summer practicing with Ram Dass. When someone asked him about vegetarianism, he said, "What comes out of your mouth is more important than what goes into it."

Communication—the listening, asking, and responding involved in verbal exchanges—is one of the most revealing mirrors of our blind spots. The challenge is so great that over half of zen's precepts are applicable to speech. Maezumi Roshi said that appropriate speech needed to consider the person, place, time, and amount, relative to what is said.

The Buddha set forth specific guidelines for considerate, compassionate communication in the Abhayarajakumara Sutta, which I have on a calligraphy:

- Is it factually accurate?
- Is it necessary?
- Is it kindly intentioned?
- Is it beneficial to all concerned?
- Is it timely?

The word *communication* shares a root with *communion,* a reminder that communication can express our inherent unity—or quite the opposite, depending on how we speak to one another. When we're upset, our clarity and aspiration are clouded, and we need to know what we're bringing to the conversation to keep our communications as transparent and empathic as possible. That's why the mental and emotional dimensions of heartmind, the hotbed of identity, preceded this section.

Some general rules can help defuse potentially difficult communication. Our first stop is to check in with ourselves, to know what thoughts and emotions are running, so they don't run amok. The next stop is to speak with the person or persons involved, as skillfully as possible. If this hits a snag, our next option is to talk with someone who can serve as a constructive resource. Our common alternatives, gossip, griping, and dumping, aren't included.

It can be helpful, before difficult exchanges, to review our aspiration to express our wish for wakefulness, starting with the conversation that is about to ensue. This might take the form of a silent practice phrase such as: "May this communication bring conscious, compassionate awareness to our communications and inspire our mutual determination to awaken from the self-centered dream."

Another helpful reminder is to keep the three primary precepts on the back (or front) burner, as they relate to communication:

1. Refrain from communicating harmfully.
2. Communicate beneficially.
3. Communicate insofar as possible in ways that reflect our fundamental interconnectedness. (Note: this doesn't mean sounding zenny.)

20 *Service Practice*

UNIFYING SELF
AND OTHERS

The best use of life is to use it—up.

M. T. HEAD

S ERVICE AND GENEROSITY have long been considered essentials in religion: Judaism's mitzvahs, or acts of kindness; Christianity's
emphasis on charity; Islam's giving of alms to the poor, a pillar of faith;
and Buddhism's *dana,* or generosity, one of six qualities of awakening. The
Roman Catholic Missionaries of Charity choose service to the poorest as
their vocation, and their group leader is called chief servant. Zen's Meal
Verse reminds us that we eat to stop all harming, to practice serving, and
to wake up.

One of the main inspirations for students of zen, academia, and life is to see the fruition of a life of service. During my decade-long collaboration with Mother Rosa Parks—whether we were attending international events, going to church, going to classes in our partner schools, or even going to my own college classes—she dramatically demonstrated her applied Christian faith. The fusion of character, determination, patience, and loving-kindness is the kind of transformation that can be precipitated by juxtaposing a hard life and engaged spiritual practice. She often spoke of the need to deepen spirituality through service, her vision undimmed (even though she couldn't see very well) by travails like death threats and fire bombings. Nothing deterred her insistence on serving youth and on founding the Rosa and Raymond Parks Institute, despite her fragile health at the time. Before she came to town, I would always set up an appointment for her with my Chinese doctor. Then she would arrive and say, "Oh, I'm fine, let's go visit the children."

One of the most remarkable examples of her indefatigability despite adversity came after a crack addict mugged her in her home, having broken in to look for money. When I called the next day, she said, "My body is bruised, but my spirit is strong. I'll be back with the children in a few weeks." Later, when the attacker was accosted for hurting her, she insisted that he not be harmed, since revenge is no solution.

Her often-stated motto, "I'll do as much as I can for as long as I can, and I hope you will too," is reflected in the motto of our local Institute: "It's always what one person can do, and that person is you." The Institute's volunteer musicians demonstrate this by producing benefit concerts in the United States, in Mexico, and on tribal nation lands in San Diego County, as well as contributing their music to CDs that are donated to youth programs. Many report that the satisfaction far exceeds professional recognition and remuneration alone.

Well-loved musicians like Harry Belafonte, the Neville family, and Sting have been generous in sharing their talents, and have been acknowledged with Rosa Parks Institute "Artists Who Serve" awards for using their talents to support compassionate action in the world. The Cyril Neville song "Sister Rosa" was performed by family members when Mother Parks inaugurated the West Coast branch.

Other premiere musicians have given generously of their time. One week I played in concerts with both guitarist Pepe Romero (who introduced me to meditation) and Igor Kipnis, longtime Rosa Parks Institute volunteer, and they offered to come to my classes at the University of California San Diego. They both remembered how much it meant to them, as young artists, when renowned musicians showed an interest in them. We all joked around and played "Chopsticks Slapstick Style," and Pepe and Igor had the students rolling in the aisles with their anecdotes. No stuffed shirts in their closets.

When service practice extends into areas we've previously considered off-limits, it can challenge and expand our comfort envelope. To broaden the limited scope of my own lifestyle, I trained as a hospice volunteer after the passing of three of my "mothers"—my own, Ezra's, and Mother Parks.

Service or community practice shouldn't be romanticized. If it were a surefire remedy for egocentrism, the term "helping professional" wouldn't be followed by the word "burnout" so often. There's also a big gap between practicing and preaching, which Ram Dass describes in *How Can I Help* (Alfred Knopf, 1988). He describes being so caught up in his writing that when he went to the store to get paper, he didn't stop for a one-legged hitchhiker because he was too busy writing a book on helping!

Still, the innumerable benefits of service outweigh the potential misuses. Albert Schweitzer said that those who will be really happy are those who seek and find ways to serve. Even if we start out believing that we are serving others, at some point it dawns on us: others are central to our lives because there are no others.

Koans of Identity and Conditioning

For eight years my formal zen practice centered around koans. During that time I recovered from being an emotional stuffer and was flooded with the emotional detritus that had been percolating under my window dressing for years. How could koan study help clarify this mess, I wondered? Scanning the fifteen hundred or so koans in the system Hakuin devised, more than half of which had already gobbled me up whole, only a handful seemed to have clear-cut applicability to the emotional and egocentric stuff that longtime meditators know so well. Still, the koan process was of inestimable value, and I determined to return to it later, to explore the possibility of utilizing koans to clarify the trained parrot's conditioning and identity. It is essential that we encounter the insubstantiality of this identity, the aggregates of the self, and realize that this "I" that is so handy for language and interacting is as devoid of solidity as everything else.

The koan process, as applied here, is a fast track for allowing the "I" to resume its role as a function and convenience without the need to be a self-assigned image. One koan that helps us to see our identity and conditioning is "Hide yourself in a person," based on the classic koan "Hide yourself in a pillar." Now, pillars are one thing; no one has ever been criticized by a pillar. But what about people? Or ourselves?

The process here, as with many koans, is to experience conscious immersion in something we usually regard as other than self. But we will start by putting ourselves into the person we think we know best, our self.

This approach doesn't reach the full scope of koan practice, but it does provide a toe-in-the-water sense of the continuum that extends from isolation through empathy to nonduality. Prerequisites for koans of conditioning and identity include thought echoing, the observer function, and the ability to feel our posture, facial expression, and overall demeanor physiologically—the experiencer function.

Hide Yourself in a Person: Studying the Self from Within

Take about a minute or less for each of the following steps:

1. *Demeanor and style.* Picture yourself in your most familiar image and demeanor. Take on this role, as a character actor playing yourself, as objectively as possible.

2. *State of mind.* What mind-set is customary for this character? Assume it as best you can.

3. *Physical stance.* Take on this character's most familiar bodily deportment.

4. *Facial expression.* Let this personality's facial expression come over your features.

5. Tone of voice. Hear the vocal inflection that characterizes this character's speech. Speak it, aloud or silently, listening carefully.

6. Classic comments. What statements is this identity likely to make? Say one, aloud or silently, now.

7. Full being. Pause briefly to feel the total experience of this character named you.

8. The world stage. Include your surroundings briefly before concluding.

Exchanging Oneself for Another: A Meditation in Empathy

After some experience with the native terrain of yourself, you might try stepping into another person, insofar as possible. We're told not to judge someone unless we've walked a mile in their shoes; in truth, life is far more than a mile, nor are we psychic, yet this small gesture can at least teach us how little we know our brother or sister.

You are now assigned the role of compassionate character actor, setting aside your own self-identity. For this exercise, choose someone who isn't too perplexing. The exercise can go badly if we fall into subjective mental commentaries about the person. Follow the same steps as before:

1. Demeanor and style. Picture this person's most familiar image and demeanor. Take on this role, as objectively as possible.

2. State of mind. What mind-set is customary for this character? Assume it as best you can while refraining from being judgmental.

3. Physical stance. Take on this character's most familiar bodily deportment.

4. *Facial expression.* Let this personality's facial expression come over your features.

5. *Tone of voice.* See if you can recall or hear the vocal inflection that characterizes this character's speech.

6. *Classic comments.* What statements is this person likely to make?

7. *Full being.* Pause briefly to feel this character's total experience.

I've often been surprised that what comes up differs greatly from my notions about the person. This doesn't mean that I've magically connected to the person; after all, we're already connected. However, some of the customary filters I usually apply, when thinking about the person, are remarkably absent.

We are reminded to ask others how they see things rather than assume we already know. Probably it's best not to mention this exercise to others. Always, motivation is central; connection and empathy, rather than analysis or control, are the purpose of this exercise.

Seamless Practice: Wholehearted Awakening

There's a joke about someone who was looking for a religion with the Ten Suggestions. We've had far more than that in these pages, and as we come closer to the end that is an eternal beginning, it's time to review some of the things that can help make awareness more seamless. Seamlessness doesn't mean we now adopt some noble ideal about being aware around the clock; fortunately, life is already seamless, even if awareness isn't. With some reminders, awareness can begin to weave from the freeways to the family, from schmoozing to sitting.

The items below are based on suggestions from this text, in roughly the order in which they appeared in previous chapters:

- Aspire to remember that a key point of zen practice is to awaken wholeheartedly to whatever is unfolding.
- Remember now, vow, how, bow: being present, vowing to awaken to our compassionate nature, knowing what approaches are effective, and cultivating the capacity for appreciation.
- Question what awakening requires in relation to what's most important.
- Cultivate the seeds of heartmind and recognize which ones can stand some tending.
- Practice the Loving-Kindness meditation to cultivate compassionate connectedness.
- Practice chest-centered awareness, particularly noticing the breath in this area, a welcome mat for the seeds of awakening.
- Develop a comprehensive practice, remembering that applied awareness calls for different approaches in different situations.
- Reflect on WIPITS (what is practice in this situation?), the mantra of a comprehensive practice.
- Remember that awareness isn't either-or; it's always *and*. Check the five dimensions of heartmind to see what's out of sight: physical, mental, emotional, open awareness, or the full-empty dimension.
- Read the body as a barometer; our body functions as a sensing instrument to help counter its long-standing task as housing an ego, and allow life's symphony to play through it.
- Keep it physical; the koan "What is this, right now?" invites our attention back to the physicality of sensations and senses.

- In sitting, remember the following:

  > Sit still, be silent, and stay put for a while.
  > Float and sink (agree with gravity).
  > Inflate and deflate (feel the body-breathing-environment as one).
  > Flow like underwater seaweed (feel the body's imperceptible flow and fluctuation).

- Notice sounds near and far, inviting attention to expand into the wide-open spaces, all the way to the horizon.
- Know that air is our ally: when confusion arises as to where awareness belongs, how about including air? Air pervades our breathing and the environment, providing evidence of life's interconnectedness.
- Keep mindfulness on the move; walking and other activities become meditation when awareness is present.
- Maintain open awareness (as developed through the Dual Awareness meditation) to keep things spacious, with room for whatever comes along.
- Keep practice practical, staying grounded in the monastery of daily living.
- Hear your trained parrot's soundtrack, and distinguish it from necessary thinking.
- Recognize your most believed thought in a given situation. If uncertain, ask: "What would I like to have said?" or "What am I most afraid of?"
- Get to know your many me's, and recognize which of them is currently vying for CWO, chief wave of the ocean. Ask, "Who do I think I am right now?"
- Grow up, wake up; growing up is a prerequisite to waking up.

- Detox the emotional dimension to bring transparency to your emotional reactivity.
- Practice three breaths of awareness, no matter what the situation may be.
- Remember that disheartenment can be a path of awakening.
- Consider that false hope leads to false hopelessness; compassionate disillusionment is necessary.
- Declare a ceasefire on the war on reality: allow, let it be; what we oppose usually resists our efforts to be rid of it.
- Remember that the vast emptiness we may be seeking is always right here, taking the form of whatever is present.
- Reflect on these aspiration boosters, vows, and practice phrases—choosing reminders of what's most important. These can be stated before meditation—to counterbalance the ego's focus on seeking comfort and maintaining inertia.
- Know the importance of guideposts like the precepts, which remind us that we can function as one, even if we don't get it yet.
- Consider that if we're seeking enlightenment, we can start with lightening up.
- Never underestimate the almost incomprehensible persistence of the power of conditioned now.

21 *Delusion Is Enlightenment*

We would rather be ruined than changed;
We would rather die in our dread
Than climb the cross of the moment
And watch our illusions die.

W. H. AUDEN

A MAN WAS DRIVING down a deserted country road and had a flat tire. When he tried to change it, he discovered his tire iron was missing. Walking toward lights in the distance, assuming it was a house, he thought, "They probably don't have a tire iron." After a mile he thought, "Maybe they'll sic their Doberman on me." Entering the driveway, he decided they were probably militia members and would shoot him. When he knocked, a woman opened the door, smiled pleasantly, and said, "Can I help you?" He yelled, "You can keep your damn tire iron!"

ᴵelusion. We look at something, a polite greeting, and see

g else: our paranoid radar screen. Delusion reverses an old

ᴺnd declares: "If I hadn't believed it, I wouldn't have seen it," which

ᴼolling Stones nailed when they sang that we're practiced at the art of

ᴇeption. When we take our unexamined thinking as fact, it becomes a

justification to act, completing the move from deluded thoughts to de-

luded action.

Delusion isn't an enemy to be destroyed; it's only a smudge on our viewpoint, but it keeps us from seeing what's in front of our face. It's tempting to hope we can annihilate all of this by getting enlightened. Yet if we're hoping for solace through what we conceive of as an altered state, we may fail to notice that we're already in one! It's this altered state that smudges our vision, so we need to make the move from delusion to disillusionment, and watch our illusions die.

Fortunately, a classic zen koan addresses this pickle: "Delusion is enlightenment; enlightenment is delusion." Here's an example. Shortly after starting zen practice, I got a free ride, one of those spontaneous instants where space and time don't apply. My assigned meditation technique at the time was counting breaths, and somewhere between six and seven, things landed in the numberless absolute. Everything known was wiped out in a swoop, yet nothing was lacking, nothing was anything, everything was utterly ordinary. The lesson was that perceptions can be overturned instantly. In fact, someone told me at the time that I'd had an enlightenment experience, which pleased me greatly. That's delusion. There's no telling how moments like that happen—and then un-happen. The path of awakening seems to be "Now you see it, now you don't," like driving through a stunning landscape that is periodically obscured by low cloud cover.

I know of no better explanation for the periodic lifting of the veil of illusion than grace, since no personal virtue is involved. Glimpses of unbounded existence come unbidden, with or without spiritual practice, even to those who aren't so nice. As Bodhidharma pointed out, acquaintance with scriptures isn't necessary either; though with thoroughgoing practice, we could write them, which is how they got written in the first place.

One thing that helps us appreciate the endeavors of those who have persevered in spiritual practice is to continue undergoing the process of disillusionment ourselves. Unpacking our fantasies about enlightenment in no way diminishes our gratitude and respect for the inspiring, compassionate practitioners whose titles or positions indicate spiritual insight. Commonsense observation shows that some people are more awake, more of the time, than others; still, we can't presume to know the heart of another. Consider how daunting it is to know the heart beating within our own breast.

If vast empty skies appear periodically, do we need to put a label on such occurrences? Words like enlightenment, *kensho,* or satori, no matter how noble, readily entice the ego to take a bow. If there seems to be a legitimate reason to mention such occurrences, why not call them openings or small glimpses into the natural order of things? And while we're at it, how about replacing the term "awake person" with "awake moments"? Attributing permanence to an impermanent state or person can cause all sorts of grief. Besides, those who are the most awake probably wouldn't object if we didn't mention it.

I once asked a teacher how long it would take me to achieve enlightenment, and he asked how long it had taken me to get as deluded as I was. Thirty-three years. Grinning, he said it probably wouldn't take that long. Fortunately, delusion is the primary catalyst that propels us into zen practice, and if we didn't have a little angst, we might just be content to eat chips and watch television forever, but how satisfying are they as a steady diet?

So if and when free rides come along, there's a price. The price of freedom, according to Zen ancestor Ikkyu, is to pay attention, pay attention, pay attention. Like zen folks everywhere, he spoke in triplicate, which makes sense when you consider the multiplicity of vistas of the physical, mental, emotional, open awareness, and full-empty dimensions.

Lighten Up

The tears I shed yesterday have become rain.
THICH NHAT HANH

In the early days of my zen practice, I once went to see one of my teachers, Zen ancestor Maezumi Roshi, in the throes of a melodrama. Listening respectfully to my woeful tale, with a Mona Lisa smile he said, "This would be tragic, if it weren't hilarious." No one had ever said anything like that to me before, at least not to my face. Other similar exchanges have deepened my appreciation for twelfth-century Tibetan teacher Longchenpa's words about how, since everything is illusory, being exactly what it is and not influenced by our views about it, we might as well burst out laughing. What a refreshing alternative to viewing spirituality as a terminally serious venture, since profundity and lightness of heart are perfectly capable of joining hands.

Thich Nhat Hanh often mentions that suffering is not enough, a point underscored by the Buddha's Noble Truths. The First Truth, which points out the ill-being and disequilibrium that pervade life, is counterbalanced by the Third and Fourth Noble Truths, which remind us that life can be viewed, and lived, very differently from that.

Suffering, grace, and wonder are not separate. So lightening up our inaccurate views of life is a significant aspect of traversing the continuum from endarkenment to an enlightening life. An elderly man with a huge sack on his back wretchedly wandered the mountains of Asia. One day, seeing a sage approaching, he cried out, "Can't you see that I'm suffering? I beg you, please help me achieve enlightenment!" The sage said, "Put down your sack." The miserable fellow replied, "No way! That I will not do." How does the story end? The answer is up to each of us.

Acknowledgments

THIS VOLUME IS DEDICATED to the memory of my parents, Helen and Clint Hamilton. My dad, a combat pilot in three wars, retired to work for peace. Now his ashes accompany me to annual Veteran Retreats with Thich Nhat Hanh. My mother's encouragement of my music helped activate the sense of determination that underwrites ongoing practice and the efforts involved in this book. How can thankfulness be expressed for the gift of life?

Mother Rosa Parks, to whom these pages are also dedicated, has had an unparalleled impact on my life. In 1955, when she was taking a stand by staying seated on a bus, my family moved to the deep South and I encountered segregation firsthand. In 1992, I invited Mother Parks to San Diego, and she, Elaine Steele, Anita Peek, and I cofounded the West Coast–Mexico branch of the Rosa and Raymond Parks Institute for Self-Development. Later, Mother Parks visited the Zen Center of San Diego and authorized it as headquarters for this branch, a gesture typical of her broad-spectrum Christian spirituality. Many exercises in this book were first used in volunteer trainings and workshops for the institute from Canada to Mexico.

Closer to home, my immeasurable gratitude and love go to Ezra Bayda, my practice partner, husband, teacher, and playmate. Living, loving, learning, and teaching together has blurred these boundaries, and his insightful comments have been a great boon to this manuscript. While I have been privileged to learn with many great teachers, Ezra shines forth in his unwavering wish to use his teachings and writings to deepen his ongoing practice. A joy of joining lives with Ezra is the bonus of daughters Jenessa and Mollie.

My first teacher, unforgettably, if intermittently, was Soen Nakagawa Roshi. Our limited contact still reverberates, with appreciation for his tenderly pointed, unerring tutelage.

Taizan Maezumi Roshi, a Zen pioneer in the United States, guided and encouraged my fledgling practice, and he graciously officiated over my undertaking of zen's precepts. He understood my aspiration to function as a life-monk, or monk of life, which was described in these pages.

Irrevocable love and gratitude are extended to my primary teacher of over two decades.

Of the many wonderful teachers I've been privileged to practice with over the years, some who particularly inspire gratitude are:

Pema Chödrön, for her relentless yet lighthearted investigation of the nooks and crannies of the path. Her willingness to share her own process as part of her teaching is a great motivation for students. So was her enthusiastic participation, as a practitioner, in the retreat that she invited Ezra and me to facilitate at Gampo Abbey. Surely this ability to demonstrate ceaseless learning is among the greatest teachings.

Thich Nhat Hanh, for many years of retreats, in conjunction with his engaged spirituality, a heartening reminder of the importance of joining the formal and applied aspects of practice.

Stephen and Ondrea Levine's presence, team example, books, and workshops underpin my exploration of service practice and loving-kindness as mainstays of the path. Ram Dass continues to open windows, starting with a three-month retreat some years ago, his books, and his example of equanimity in the midst of changing life circumstances. Toni Packer's direct, Socratic approach stimulates an ongoing spirit of inquiry.

Jon Kabat-Zinn's founding of the Center for Mindfulness in Medicine, Health Care, and Society, and programs in mindfulness-based stress reduction, have inspired my teaching and volunteer efforts. His personal encouragement, example of family practice with Myla, and insistence on coloring outside the lines of conventional spiritual venues are catalysts that remind us of the full field of spiritual practice.

Many colleagues and friend practitioners kindle inspiration. Special appreciation for support in recent times goes to Diane Eshin Rizzetto, Gregg Howard, Geoff Dawson, Barry Magid, Roshi Wendy Egyoku Nakao, Roshi Nicolee Jikyo Miller McMahon, Roshi Jan Chozen Bays, Roshi Anne Seisen Saunders, Steve Hagen, Roshi James Ishmael Ford, Josh Bartok, Diana Devitt Dawson, and Roshi Nelson Foster. Episcopal priest Father Brian Taylor encouraged my exploration of spiritual interfaces by encouraging me to facilitate retreats with his Christian Zen mediation group in Albuquerque. My friends from the Ordinary Mind Zen School are affectionately appreciated.

Others whose influence has been strong include Marshall Rosenberg, a ten-year mentor in compassionate communication; the Onodaga Nation chief, Joagquisho Oren Lyons, of the Iroquois Federation, for putting an inspiring face on democracy; Robert Johnson, who opened the unlocked door to the inner world; Dr. Howard Gardner, whose multiple intelligence approach is transforming education and my teaching in all venues; Chancellor Constance Carroll, for modeling what is possible in academia; Dr. David Reynolds, for training in Naikan and Morita practice; Bill Moyers, Rosa Parks Award recipient; Donna Varnau; Jim and Lois Lasry; John Ankele; and Anthony and Mary Jane Newman.

Many chi kung teachers have helped enliven the energetic interplay of movement and stillness. Particular thanks go to Sifu Share K. Lew and Carol Elliott, L.Ac.

Words fall short in expressing my thanks to the hospice community for their service in the life and death of both my mother, Helen, and Ezra's mother, Mollie, and the powerful training they have provided for accompanying those whose life energy is declining.

Special thanks to Barbara Sullivan, Wendy Maland, Linda Dydyk, and Jenessa Bayda, who practically digested the contents. Others who test-drove the material are Robert Amedeo, Halifa Ayshegul Ashki Al-Jerrahi, Punit Auerbacher, Robin Cooney, Judy Oberlander, Larry Parker, Jodi Reed, Laura Urquhart, Justin Weaver, and others who come for retreats from around the world.

Let's not forget M. T. Head, for providing me with a pseudonym and for supporting occasional rap efforts like the Hiphop Heart Sutra and the Funk-adelic Morning Verse. I sometimes have to call M.T. my "altar ego," since zen is big on altars, and to shake up a certain curmudgeonly and iconoclastic streak.

Emily Bower has been more than an editor. Her unstinting efforts have helped midwife this offering in coming forth, with patience, encouragement, and a serendipitous combination of language skills and strong spiritual practice that have helped tame my penchant for turning a haiku into the *Iliad*. Ben Gleason's additional editorial efforts and good cheer have been a great help, going beyond what was expected. The invisible copyeditors and the Shambhala family's group effort has guided my efforts to convey verbally the unity of zen's seemingly mystifying aspects and the relative reality in which they are garbed.

As a zen meal verse says, "Seventy-two labors brought us this food; may we appreciate how it comes to us." Limitless influences remain unacknowledged despite their indispensable collaboration in the fruition of this endeavor and our shared existence.

With appreciation, Elizabeth Hamilton

Index of Exercises and Checklists

About the Author

E LIZABETH HAMILTON TEACHES and lives at the Zen Center of San Diego with her husband and practice partner, Ezra Bayda. She leads zen retreats and programs throughout the United States and Hawaii, Australia, and Canada. She has published numerous articles and dharma teachings under the pen name M. T. Head.

Elizabeth and Mother Rosa Parks cofounded the San Diego–Mexico branch of the Rosa Parks Institute in 1992 and worked together for many years. Elizabeth has also studied and practiced qigong as moving meditation for seventeen years.

For more information about Elizabeth's and Ezra's teachings and the Zen Center of San Diego, go to www.zencentersandiego.org.